D1022021

Lessons to My Children

Simple Life Lessons for Financial Success,
Wealth and Abundance

By I. Mark Cohen, J.D., LL.M, CFP® and
Weston D. Burnett, J.D., LL.M, CFP®

Copyright © 2010 I. Mark Cohen and Weston D. Burnett

All rights reserved.
No part of this book may be used or reproduced in any manner
whatsoever without written permission of the publisher.

Library of Congress Control Number: 2010927895
ISBN 0-9802118-7-5

Books are available for special promotions and premiums.
For details, contact Special Markets, LINX, Corp., Box 613,
Great Falls, VA 22066, or e-mail specialmarkets@linxcorp.com

Book design by Paul Fitzgerald
Editing by Sandra Gurvis
Published by LINX

LINX, Corp.
Box 613
Great Falls, VA 22066
www.linxcorp.com

Printed in the United States of America

Dedication

To Our Wonderful Clients and Our Families,
including Grandparents, Parents, Wives, Children
and Grandchildren-to-be

LESSONS TO MY CHILDREN

Acknowledgements

Our joint firms – Navigator Wealth Management, a financial services firm, and Cohen and Burnett, PC, our law firm – are blessed with the finest clients. They are intelligent, successful in life, and full of love. Serving them is a pleasure. Learning from them has enriched us in ways that lead us to want to pass on the lessons that we observed in them and in our own families.

We wish to proudly acknowledge the parts played by those at Navigator Wealth Management and Cohen and Burnett, PC. First and foremost is Susan Greco who moved us from talking about a book to the reality. Without her, this book would still just be an idea waiting to be born. Nicci Yang is our consummate webmaster. Lawrence Solomon is our consummate financial expert who provided editorial and substantive suggestions. Andrew Vanderhoof, Senior Associate Counsel, provided constructive edits. To the rest of the staff of Navigator and Cohen & Burnett, PC, thank you for helping us take care of our clients while freeing us to work on this book.

We are very grateful to our publisher, Steve Eunpu, and his team at LINX for leading us expertly through the publishing process with such quality work and advice. And to Brigette Polmar, we are thankful for her expert guidance on getting the word out about LTMC.

As always we thank our families for all they have done for us. Our parents and grandparents taught us these lessons through their lives. Mark's children, Michael and Rachel, and Wes' children, David, Edward, his fiancée Alka Pradhan, and Jennifer and her husband J.D. Beard, contributed stories, anecdotes and lessons learned throughout this book. Finally, for Mark's wife Kathy and Wes' wife Barbara, we owe a debt of gratitude for their patience and support.

TABLE OF CONTENTS

LESSONS TO MY CHILDREN

FOREWORD:
Lessons From Their Children

By Michael Cohen and David Burnett

Small things matter, and big things have little beginnings.

When our fathers, the co-authors of this book, Mark Cohen and Wes Burnett, asked us to share some of our thoughts and experiences while they were writing this book on financial literacy and abundance, we each began to think of the practical wisdom they shared with us over the years and can summarize it in a few words: "start now," patience, save, and self-discipline.

Start Now

But you may hear yourself saying or thinking, "I know I should be doing this stuff but I can't possibly get started now. I am too busy and not quite making ends meet. I am buried in debt and bills. My paycheck is like rain in the desert – it evaporates before it hits the ground! I can't possibly start saving now. I will have to wait until I get a raise or a better job."

But here's a fact of life. Regardless of how much or how little you earn, you can reorganize your life to pretty much control where you money is going. It takes commitment to start, some up-front work, and about five minutes per day to stay organized and on budget.

This one lesson – start now – is the most important of all because the information imparted in the Lessons of this book are useless in the absence of motivation. If you think your life it too hectic to start now, how – and when – is that going to change? There is never a "convenient" time for changes – to quote John Lennon, "life is what happens while you are busy making other plans."

Michael's Lessons

Patience

The first financial lesson I remember came to me when I was about five years old. I saw my friends on the bus playing with this red, shiny monster-like doll, with all sorts of cool features that put my Legos and Lincoln Logs to shame. I loved it. I had to have it. And I let my mom and dad know, day and night, that this was *the* toy and that I wanted it more than anything else. They either got the picture or just wanted to put an end to my incessant whining and took me to a toy store where, lo and behold, the toy was on the shelf with a price-tag that made my dad raise his eyebrow and ask me, "You really want this toy, Michael?"

"Yes!"

"Let's see how much you want it in two weeks."

I left the store empty-handed and disappointed. But two weeks later I was no longer pining for that toy, and so I came away with an appreciation for how important it is to give yourself time to think about a purchase, especially a major one, before you go ahead and make it. I use this time to think about how much I really want the item, whether it's worth the money, or whether I can get it or something comparable in other places for less money. The idea isn't to prevent me from buying it altogether, but to make sure I give myself enough time to think about the issue and not let the "gotta have it" impulse win the day.

Save

Basically, my parents encouraged my sister and I to automatically put away at least 10 percent of whatever we earned. It's a simple principle, but the benefits are manifold. First, you're always saving something. Second, you are becoming accustomed to working with a reduced budget. Third, when you retire or cease to have a regular income, you'll have trained yourself to spend your savings more wisely and frugally, because you've been spending something less than your full income all along.

This lesson borders on another simple lesson: little things add up, or, big things have small beginnings. The idea is that a little bit of savings, if practiced regularly and diligently can, over time, amount to something significant. On the other hand, a regular habit of buying Starbucks coffee, will, and probably in relatively short time, also add up to a large amount of money. It works both ways.

Self-Discipline

You don't need to be a financial wizard to save, but you do need self-discipline to have your money work for you. This means having the ability to continually hold oneself to a regimen, plan, or principle undistracted by opportunities for short-term gain or quick impulse satisfaction. It means thinking over the long term and keeping that vision even when it's difficult, not immediately helpful, or frustrating. Self-discipline is a challenge, but it's important for finances and virtually any undertaking in life. Fundamentally, self-discipline is learned not from books or pithy sayings but from diligent practice in everyday life.

David's Lessons

Savings

I was aware from a young age that it was more important to save money than to spend money, since it was important to have savings for large future expenses (such as college and down payments, in particular) and to one day provide for one's own children and grandchildren.

Good Habits

We grew up in an era before the American savings rate dipped below zero, when – at least in our family – good financial habits were passed down from generation to generation, and saving for the future was understood to be a duty to self and family. I was aware as a child that my parents and grandparents had selflessly provided for me, financially, by setting aside money during my entire childhood to be used later in life to pay for education and other things. I'm grateful to my parents and grandparents for planning that far in advance and for making personal sacrifices to provide for the next generations. The money they saved and invested paid, at least in part, for high school, college, grad school, law school, and beyond. I was aware of those savings as a child because my parents reminded us of them and of the importance of saving.

All About Money and Planning for the Future

The way my parents spoke about those savings instilled in me a few important lessons: 1) money is something to be saved rather than spent on luxuries or other unimportant things; 2) savings are something to be invested for your own future, and for the future of your family; 3) I have my parents, grandparents, and great-grandparents to thank for giving me a good foundation in life, both through education and affection and support but also by planning ahead financially and providing for me; 4) one does not have to be rich, or have a high income, to save a lot and have that money accumulate over time, due to the power of compounded earnings and interest; 5) good financial habits–living within one's means, saving for the future, thinking of your children and their children – are something that can be passed on through the generations; 6) spend money where it will maximize value (such as on school where it will provide an excellent education and thereby help young people later in life) and do not spend on less important things (like luxury cars or wardrobes); 7) money should be a means to an end. It was for us as children. I do not remember being terribly aware of money, status, or wealth as a child. I thank my parents for shielding me from a more commercial, materialistic lifestyle. What was more important was being around family, reading, playing outside, exercising, doing well in school, applying myself to Boy Scouts and Cub Scouts and other activities, being around friends, taking family vacations and holidays, etc.

It is our hope that our fathers' words will provide some insight and ideas as you read these Lessons and embark upon your journey to financial security and effective money management.

Michael Cohen, age 21 is the son of author Mark Cohen and is a full time student at the College of William and Mary in Williamsburg, VA.

David Burnett, age 32, is the son of author Wes Burnett and is an associate at a large New York law firm.

LESSONS TO MY CHILDREN

INTRODUCTION

Financial Literacy: Knowledge Is Wealth

When you are young, you have an asset that's even more powerful than money – time. As with most things in life, you can use your time wisely or squander it. The sooner in life that you learn how to manage your money, the more wealth and financial security you will accumulate. You don't have to be rich or even reasonably well-off, just motivated to follow the information in these lessons regularly and consistently. And you can start at any time, but now is best.

What Is Financial Literacy?

When you are young, your parents pay for your food, clothing, and shelter. In many cases you are given an allowance to spend on things you want, like treats and toys. So money may not be something you think a lot about. However, in order to function in society and lead a relatively stress-free and enjoyable life, you'll need to learn how to handle and manage money. And the sooner you start thinking about where your money goes and how to save it, the better. When times are tough, you will know how to manage your finances to avoid overextending your credit or bankruptcy. You'll also have enough money put aside to get you through job loss, illness, or other unexpected misfortunes. So, as with anything in life – be it brushing your teeth, exercising, and eating healthy foods – the sooner you start to develop good habits, the better.

The art of understanding and managing your money is known as **financial literacy**. It enables you to make financial decisions that will benefit you now and in the future. Another way of looking at financial literacy is about knowing the language of success.

Once you speak "financial literacy" you can:

- Save money for short and long-term goals
- Manage and balance a budget
- Use credit responsibly and minimize debt
- Understand taxes and how to best deal with them
- Manage financial risks and investing.

Financial literacy is important, and since there are few courses about it in school, this book will help fill the gap.

How to Use This Book

The Lessons are designed to guide one step-by-step through the various aspects of money management. Each lesson is self-contained so you can refer back to it if you have specific questions or need more information. Lessons 1 and 2 provide the basics of how to save, paying yourself first, and understanding how wealth can accumulate over time. Lessons 3-5 offer specifics on money management – living within your budget, having a financial plan, and limiting debt. Lessons 6 and 7 will help you get the most out of your money by understanding how to evaluate what you're paying for and balancing risk and reward. The last four Lessons, 8, 9, 10, and 11, are the "nuts and bolts" of investing, finding the right experts to guide you, keeping and organizing records, and understanding taxes.

If you purchased this book to learn the principles of sound financial judgment, read on. If you are looking to pass these principles for financial success onto another, then hand the book over to that young adult you know. Alternately, you might use the information contained here as a framework to start that conversation with your own children or another young adult you care enough about to give them the best possible financial start.

Taken together or separately, these Lessons will provide a beacon to guide you through the sometimes tumultuous sea of finances. As with life itself, the waters can be smooth or choppy. However, with the information in these Lessons, not only will you be able to weather any storm, but you'll likely come out full speed ahead with regard to saving, investing, and money management.

LESSONS TO MY CHILDREN

LESSON 1

Pay Yourself First

What is not started today is never finished tomorrow.

Johann Wolfgang von Goethe

You are your own greatest asset. If you invest in yourself by getting an education and maintaining good health through exercise and eating well, you reap the rewards throughout life. The same is true of finances. So when you receive that first paycheck, rather than asking how much is left over for movies, dinners out, and clothes after rent, gas, and living expenses are paid, consider how much to "invest" in yourself through saving for the future. Because the more you save, the more self-reliant and self-sustaining you become, through both good times and bad.

Justin's Story

I married Laura the week after she graduated from college and right after I finished my first year of law school. We'd either lived in our parents' homes or college dorm rooms, but never on our own. Even though my law school tuition took up a huge chunk of her first-year teacher's salary, by mid-June we had a fourth-floor walk up apartment, wedding presents, clothes and books, but no furniture. So Laura spent our wedding money on the bed, a chest of drawers, a nightstand, and a sofa, all for 50 percent off. For $5 we bought a well-used sideboard for all the wedding present silver, and for the eating area we borrowed two living room chairs from my grandparents and a drop-leaf table and four chairs from my great-aunt and uncle.

Although we had no money, we also had no debt, and paid for everything with cash or check. Our savings went for a used car and paying my fall tuition. Public transportation was limited so I commuted to classes by bike. Our savings was my tuition bills which was our investment in our future together.

After I graduated from law school, we had two paychecks and, although there were plenty of financial demands, we put our joint salaries into one account for family expenses, and two separate, much smaller, accounts to spend on our own for clothes, gifts or hobbies. We were still fairly frugal, but didn't need to devote time and emotional energy on debates about how to allot our funds, even when they were meager.

Why Pay Myself First?

Let's face it: It's much easier to **not** even think about a savings plan, especially when you're young. Human nature being what it is, most of us prefer the instant gratification of **impulse buying** – purchasing whatever suits our whims at a particular moment – over voluntarily denying ourselves and putting away money. So the best way to make sure you save is to automatically put funds into a savings account at the start of each pay period. If it's already allotted and you can't see it, then you won't be tempted to spend it.

Before you start saving, however, you'll need to know how much you can realistically put away. That involves setting up a **budget,** a plan involving sums of money allocated for a particular purpose, such as gas, rent, and utilities. To set up your budget you'll need your first paycheck for the full pay period. Having a complete check – whether you're paid weekly, biweekly, or monthly will give you an idea of how much money you actually have. Ideally, 90 percent of your take-home pay can be used to create the budget, with the remaining 10 percent being used for savings. See Lesson 3 for more details on setting up and living within a budget.

Figure 1.1 illustrates how much money you can accumulate over time, if you save $100 per month starting at ages 12, 16, 18, 22, and 30 (5 percent annual interest compounded monthly) ending at age 65. You can accumulate a great deal of money by saving 10 percent of each paycheck, no matter how small, as long as you do so consistently. As the chart shows, even waiting four years can make a huge difference.

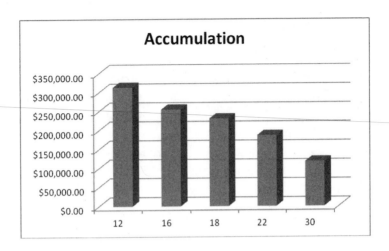

Figure 1.1. Money Accumulation Chart

Along with self-reliance and financial independence, personal savings represent freedom. Say you have a job that you hate or pays poorly, or you lose your job. With a financial safety net, you'll have room to plan if you want to resign to find something better or if you get laid off. Savings can also be a lifesaver if you get hit with unexpected bills or an illness and will give you something to fall back on.

Ruth's Story

When I started working part-time, my Dad agreed to match my earnings with a contribution of up to $2,000 per year in an individual retirement account (IRA). Although retirement was the last thing on the mind of this 16-year-old, I really liked the idea of money in the bank, so I went along with the plan. Dad would do this for the two years I worked while in high school and all the years I was in college, up to 10 total years.

However, as part of the deal, Dad asked me to figure out how much would be in my retirement account assuming I got a 10 percent annual return and there were no other contributions. I calculated that at age 65 I would have more than $1.3 million in the IRA. In other words, because of the time value of money, we invested a total of $20,000 and received back $1.3 million 49 years later. How cool was that?

Then he had me calculate how much I would accumulate if I waited 10 years to age 26 and invested $2,000 per year for every year until retirement. The answer was a real shocker – I would only have about $800,000 at retirement! I would be investing $58,000 more and getting half a million less!

Finally, he asked me to estimate how much I would have to invest every year if I were to end up with $1.3 million, but started after college at age 26. That was a little harder to do, but we calculated that I would need to invest $3,238 per year for the next 39 years, or $126,293, to accumulate $1.3 million. I had only invested $20,000 in those first 10 years, but missing those years would have cost me over $100,000 in additional savings to make up for the lost time. When it comes to investing, the early bird who saves regularly really does get the worm!

How Do I Start?

You start by determining the amount to set aside each payday. It should be equal to or greater than 10 percent of your paycheck but could be as little as 5 percent, depending upon your expenses. Then go ahead and make a budget to help you figure out your expenses relative to your income. Usually budgets are set up on a monthly basis to give you an idea of income as well as outflow of money. See Lesson 3 for details on how to make a budget work for you.

When Do I Start?

You can start anytime, but most people begin to save more seriously when they land their first full-time job. Even if you have student loans, you'll need an emergency fund so plan for that first. You'll have plenty of time to put your money in investments later.

Regardless of what you are saving for, **be consistent.** Make no exceptions. If you don't put money in every single pay period, it will be too easy to fall off the wagon. Saving money should be a habit. You should save automatically with out even thinking about it.

What Should I Include and How Much?

Drop in a portion of any extra money that you get for holidays and birthdays as well as a percentage of your paychecks. This includes:

- Ideally, 10 percent of money you get after taxes (including allowances, bonuses, and gifts) per year.

- Loose change. Say you purchase coffee at work and receive change back. Put it in a "spare change bucket" to be converted to dollars at the bank or grocery when it reaches a certain point.

- After you finish paying off a debt, save that monthly payment going forward.

- Save your pay raise.

- Add an extra $100 to each month's mortgage payment.

- Put in the maximum amount allowable in your retirement accounts.

If you are fortunate enough to receive a large gift for a specific purpose; make sure all the money goes towards that particular purpose. But if someone gives you a large amount of money with no strings attached, put half towards your savings goal.

Even if you follow only a few of the above-mentioned suggestions, you are making great strides towards building financial security.

Where Do I Put the Money?

Once you have a regular job and are living on your own, your first savings priority is to accumulate an emergency fund – six months living expenses. Keep the first three month's money in a simple bank savings account or a money market fund. Both of these will allow immediate access (liquidity) and will pay some interest, albeit small. The liquidity and safety of principal are more important than return on the savings for this money.

Once you have three months' worth of living expenses in your bank or money market savings account, you might want to consider purchasing a 90-day **certificate of deposit (CD).** Purchased directly through a commercial bank or savings and loan institution, CDs are short- or medium-term, interest-bearing, and low-risk. But they tie up invested money for the duration of the certificate's maturity, which can be anywhere from three months to six years. Because your money is tied up, however, until the CD matures, they offer higher rates of return than a bank savings account.

Say you're on a (bank)roll and you have four months' worth of living expenses saved up in the bank. You can start purchasing what's known as three-month rolling CDs. These are 90-day CDs that renew automatically; each one has one month's living expenses. Once you have three of these going, you'll have six months living expenses and can move on to other types of investments, which will be discussed in Lesson 8 on investing.

However, CDs can have one major drawback. If they are cashed in before their maturity date, you give up the interest you would have earned (typically the last six months for CDs that have maturities longer than half a year). But if you have issues with impulse spending and really want to save, you might want to consider putting at least some of your money into CDs. That way, it's more difficult to get the money out and will force you to think twice about whether you actually want to buy the item.

How Do I Keep Track of Balances?

As with life itself, maintaining balances can be a tricky thing. If you ignore them, especially in a checking account, you can lose track of your money and may overdraw your funds. If you check too frequently, especially if it's a long term investment or stock market purchase, you may be disappointed and make rash decisions or be tempted to spend.

For short-term accounts, such as checking, it's a good idea to check them daily. Online checking accounts that involve a debit card are the easiest to keep track of. Every morning review what you've spent, and what hasn't yet cleared and you'll have better control of your money and upcoming expenses. Also monitor deposits and payments for accuracy and completeness.

Savings accounts (which are usually also online and tied with checking accounts) should also be reviewed regularly, although perhaps not quite as often. Not only will this provide the satisfaction of seeing your savings grow, but you can also make sure that nothing was accidentally taken out (such as bank fees) and that interest has been added correctly. Sometimes even banks can make mistakes.

TIP FOR THE PARENT: The daughter's first real job was as the "dipping girl" at a chocolate shop. It was her job to stand in the window all day and dip strawberries, orange slices, and various other things into this vat of melted chocolate. The job paid $8 an hour, much more than any of her friends were making. When she was about to start the job, her parents had her open up her first account, a checking account. All of her paychecks were going to be deposited into this account, giving her the chance, as a 16-year old, to learn how to manage an account. Before receiving her first paycheck, her dad set the rule that for each of her paychecks, she was to save half ($4/hour), and was allowed to spend the other half ($4/hour). Additionally, her dad had a creative way of getting her to understand the value of income versus the value of what she wanted to spend the money on. For example, he told her that if she wanted to buy a $24 shirt, she needed to decide whether it was worth 6 hours of work (6 hours times $4/hour).

Take This to the Bank

- Pay yourself first, before your rent or the electric company.

- Try to save 10 percent of everything you earn.

- Curb impulse buying and set up a budget.

- Make savings a priority and watch your "nest egg" grow.

- Also closely watch how much you spend, and check balances regularly.

- Consider alternative sources of savings, such as Certificates of Deposits (CDs) that will trade off liquidity for enhanced returns.

Parting Shot

When you pay yourself first, you mentally establish saving as a priority. You're telling yourself that you are more important than anyone else, even the bank that holds your mortgage or car loan or the credit card company. Paying yourself first encourages sound financial habits; your steady and regular contributions are building a cash buffer and a nest egg. Not only does paying yourself first provide you with financial freedom, but it opens up opportunities for the future.

LESSON 2

Patience Pays

The only reason for time is so that everything doesn't happen at once.

Albert Einstein

The **time value of money (TVM)** is based on the concept that the dollar you have today is worth more than the same amount received at some time in the future. If you get a dollar and invest it today with a 4 percent annual rate of return, it will be worth $1.04 in twelve months. This may not seem like a lot of money, but it can add up greatly over a period of time.

There are two reasons a dollar today is worth more than a dollar next year: (1) inflation; and (2) the earnings a dollar can make for you between today and next year. **Inflation** is where things cost more (or your dollars buy less) in the future. It is one of the biggest threats to a successful financial plan. Inflation has averaged around 3 percent, but in some years it has been as high as 10 percent. In order to counter the effect of inflation, you must make at least that amount, after taxes and expenses, on your investments. If you are making 3 percent in a CD, for example, and paying income tax on your earnings, you are netting about 2 percent after taxes, and therefore are losing purchasing power with your investment. Bank CDs, which typically will pay you the current rate of inflation, are a safe way to slowly lose purchasing power, and should be used cautiously for that reason.

The second reason a dollar today is worth more than a dollar next year is because you can make the dollar work for you right now. If you are earning 5 percent on your dollar today, you will have a dollar and five cents in a year.

TVM 101

You'll need to know and plan for the time value of money in order to know how far your dollars will go, whether it's for five or fifty years from now. As mentioned earlier, inflation averages around 3 percent annually which means that the purchasing power of your money will be cut in half every 23.5 years. So if you want to live on the income from $2 million in 23.5 years, plan on saving $4 million, and then make sure the $4 million continues to grow at 3 percent during your retirement.

Financial institutions understand the time value of money by offering to give you your money through periodic payments. They hang on to your money for as long as possible even though it may not be in your best interest – upcoming payments may be worth less due to inflation or zero, if the financial institution disappears through bankruptcy. That's why sometimes it's better to take a lump sum rather than monthly payments. However, if payouts are adjusted upwards for inflation, (sometimes known as cost of living adjustments [COLAs]) then it might be more to your benefit to choose that option. If the COLAs are at least as high as inflation, you can avoid the higher taxes of a lump sum payment.

Calculating the Time Value of Money

If a dollar today is worth a dollar and three cents in a year, then the time value of the dollar is worth three cents per year. If you can make a 10 percent return on your dollar then the time value of your dollar is 10 cents per year. There is a simple formula for the future value of your dollar that looks like this:

$$FV = PV \cdot (1+i)^n$$

Where:

PV is the present value

i is the interest rate (or rate of inflation)

n is the number of periods

For example, one dollar earning 10 percent in a year has the future value of:

$$FV = 1 \cdot (1+.10)^1 = \$1.10$$

Of course that was simple enough to do without the formula. How about our claim earlier that $2 million needs to be worth $4 million in 23.5 years to keep pace with inflation?

$$FV = 2,000,000 \cdot (1+.03)^{23.5} = \$4.006 \text{ Million}$$

The NPV – A Future-iffic Option

Another way of anticipating how much your money will be worth is to take an anticipated cash payment in the future and calculate the Net Present Value (NPV) as a lump sum today. Say after you graduate from college in five years, you plan on taking out $2,000 as a down payment on a car. How much will you need to save each month to get to $2,000 in five years?

The formula is too complicated for this book, but you can use the calculator on the book's Web site to find that, if you got a constant return of 7 percent, you would need to save $325 per year for the next five years to reach $2,000. You will find a number of useful financial calculators at this book's Web site, at www.LessonsToMyChildren.com.

Real-World Examples: TVM in Action

- Your insurance company sends you an annual renewal for your auto policy for $1,100. You can pay it all at once or in $275 increments over four months. There is no interest charge. It's best to pay it quarterly as it's less of an initial investment and the value of payments depreciate due to inflation.

- Are you better off with a 30-year mortgage or a 15-year mortgage? How about choices between interest rates? A mortgage calculator found on this book's Web site works using the same principles as the TVM formula. You can figure out the monthly payment and compare it to what you can realistically afford. Factor in how much it will cost to close the loan (closing points can also be calculated on the Web site) and you can work the variables to your advantage. Do this even before you go shopping for the house.

- Annuity calculators let you calculate any one of the five TVM variables: present value (PV), interest rate (i), period (N), your payment rate (PMT) and the future value (FV).

Traps to Avoid

- *Remember to save with an eye to inflation.* Right now you may be thinking that $1 million would be enough to support your $50,000 per year lifestyle, but when you retire 30 years from now that $1 million is only worth $400,000 in purchasing power. You will need closer to $2.5 million. People who retire on a fixed income will lose about 3 percent of their purchasing power every year. This means it will lose half of its value in about 23.5 years. So if you retire on a fixed income at age 65, you will have lost half of your purchasing power by the time you reach 88.

- *Businesses understand profit margins and take advantage of TVM.* Large companies that want to pay you off over time for an insurance settlement, annuity payout, or structured settlement do so out of self-interest, as they understand that hanging onto the money rather than paying it all at once gives them more profits. However, payouts that adjust upward for inflation are fairer to both parties, and might give you an income tax advantage.

- *Not paying off credit cards.* This detracts from the time value of money since there is an expense associated with withholding payment, namely interest. Monthly interest rates are cumulative and will cost you much more than paying off the card with the cash in your accounts.

TIP FOR THE PARENT: The child learned a lesson about inflation (and sharing) when his older brother took his full glass of lemonade, poured half of it into his little brother's empty glass, and then added water to fill both glasses up. They each had a full glass but it contained only half as much lemonade. Inflation started historically in much the same way when the king would take gold and mix in cheaper metals but still pay the same as if it were solid gold.

Take This to the Bank

- Knowledge is key. The more you understand such concepts as the time value of money and net present value, the better you will fare in major purchases or payouts.

- Money in your pocket is better than a promise that you will get it in the future.

- Keeping money in your pocket as opposed to reducing debt is more complex, since you must assess the cost of carrying that debt and compare that to the benefit of the cash.

- When investing money, always do your homework, whether it's calculating the payout on a simple interest CD or choosing among mortgage options.

- Any time there are periodic payments, the time value of money is a factor. Evaluate whether such payments are adjusted for inflation and how they will appreciate or depreciate in the future.

- Become comfortable with and familiar with TVM calculators, many of which can be found on this book's Web site.

Parting Shot

Retiring on a fixed income is like getting a 3 percent pay cut every year. After 23½ years you will only have half of what you started with. By the same token, if you are saving up for a $20,000 down payment on a house five years from now, realize that you will need about $23,000 by then.

Understanding the time value of money will help counter the negative effects of inflation. You can do more with money in your pocket now than you can with a promise that someone will give you that same amount of money in the future. A dollar today is worth more than a dollar a year from now.

LESSONS TO MY CHILDREN

LESSON 3

Write Yourself a "Reality" Check

The surest way to ruin a man who does not know how to handle money is to give him some more.

George Bernard Shaw

If you have a budget and live within it, you have peace of mind and financial security. Your increased knowledge of your total income and expenses means you are informed and organized and have asserted control over your financial life. Managing your budget is a win-win situation that translates into a steady increase of your net worth as you reduce liabilities, incur fewer new ones and add to your assets.

There's Something about Jim and Sally

Jim and Sally both have good jobs and try to be careful with their spending. They always shop around for the best price, seek sales and discounts and use coupons. However, no matter how vigilant they are, they seem to be getting further and further into debt.

How did they get into this bind? "Being careful" with money was not enough. They needed to know exactly how much they can spend based on their combined incomes. The solution is simple and relatively easy – a budget. In fact, unless you have unlimited funds, everyone needs a budget.

One of the chief reasons people reject the idea of a budget is that they do not want to limit their spending. Like Jim and Sally, you will need to get past this illogical but emotionally powerful mental block to avoid getting into debt over your head.

What Is a Budget?

In the simplest terms, a **budget** is a list of your planned income and expenses. However, in the broader scheme of things, it is also a strategic plan for how you spend your money that includes tactical decisions on what to do tomorrow.

How you use your money tomorrow is **tactical**; what you do with it over time is **strategic**. Jim and Sally in the above example are highly paid professionals but spend everything that comes in the door with very little left over. They actually cannot live within a budget since their paychecks are the only budget they can stick with. They are tactical only. But if Jim and Sally manage to save something out of each paycheck and stick to a budget that includes setting aside money, they are being strategic as well. Being both tactical and strategic is essential to managing your money effectively.

Why Create a Budget?

Phil's Story

Phil started a construction company that was an almost immediate success. Yet, he had no true grasp of what he was earning and spending. Although he won several large contracts, he ended up with ever-increasing debts, borrowing more and more against credit cards. He cashed in his retirement accounts to pay the bills and never checked to see if the withholding had been taken out for taxes. As a result, he ended up paying penalties and interest and lost a large part of his savings and retirement to legal fees and tax penalties.

Although Phil was running a business, and you may be just starting out, you can learn from his mistakes. Regardless of how you earn money, sit down and figure out exactly what you're going to need and when you'll have to spend it, factoring in 10 percent for savings. Although it's great to be able to go to the mall and spend that paycheck on the latest fad, you don't want to be caught short, if you need to pay extra withholding taxes or don't have enough saved up for living expenses. As Phil discovered, living paycheck to paycheck and not taking time to make a budget can be a recipe for disaster.

You construct a budget to avoid overspending your income. You want to match your income to your expenses so that you will "make ends meet" (and also set aside some for savings!). And the sooner you create the budget, the better. Why wait to save money? As mentioned in Lesson 2, the time value of money is very important.

Other reasons to create a budget:

- Reduces your chances for bank fees such as overdraft charges.

- Reduces the risk that you will have to borrow and pay interest and thereby increase your payments.

- Tracks expenses better and identifies excessive items you really don't need and can therefore get rid of.

Living within your budget has many benefits. If for instance, it shows a negative – that you are spending more than you're making – you can take steps to correct the deficiency by cutting out certain expenses, such as shopping and dining out. If it shows a positive cash flow, then you can save more and secure a better future for yourself.

A budget must also fit your personal circumstances. It helps you plan for near-term expenses and long-term goals. It provides a measuring stick for your financial progress. In general, a budget should be within these rule-of-thumb limits:

- Housing expense not more than 25 percent of gross income (that is, income before taxes or other deductions).

- Transportation expenses not more than 16 percent of gross income.

- Not more than 60 percent for total non-discretionary expenses including housing, transportation, taxes, food.

- That leaves 40 percent roughly for savings, entertainment, investment, and special irregular expenses.

For example, say your gross pay is $4,000 per month. The rent/mortgage should be no more than $1,000, the car and related expenses should be $640 or less. You can figure that fuel, repairs, maintenance, and car insurance will cost about $200 per month, so your car payment should be about $440. Remaining non-discretionary expenses (utilities, food, health and life insurance, etc.) should be no more than $760 per month. That leaves $400 per month for savings (10 percent) and $1,200 per month for everything else, including entertainment, vacations, hobbies, and so on.

Richard's Story

My parents made sure that we always did and had everything that we wanted, yet they still saved significant amounts of money for our education. As kids, my siblings and I watched my parents methodically plan vacations to fun and exotic places, making sure that we spent exactly as much as we needed to have a wonderful time, without wasting a dime! For example, when I was 13 we went to Disney World and of course I was determined to stay in the resort and do all of the "character breakfasts" and other events that get quite expensive. In the weeks leading up to our trip, my father and I endlessly researched the combinations of hotels/restaurants/entry tickets that would give us the optimal experience and yet remain reasonable. I did indeed get to have breakfast with Goofy, and we stayed at the Disney Beach Club Resort in beautiful lake view rooms. But along with every single detail of the trip – one of my favorite vacations ever – I can still remember every possible dining and accommodation option for the parks, with corresponding pricing. This came in quite handy when I went back to Disney World last year with my friends. Moral of this story – you can go on a budget and still get breakfast with Goofy!

How to Create a Budget

Most budgets are pretty clear-cut and generally look like this:

INCOME	
Source	
Taxable Nature (investment, wages, pension, rental)	
EXPENSES	
Taxes	
Housing	
Food	
Auto	
Insurance	
Medical/Dental	
School or Childcare	
Debt	
Entertainment	
Savings	
Investments	

Figure 3.1 Sample Spreadsheet

The most efficient way to set up a budget is to use a spreadsheet as illustrated in Figure 3.1 on the previous page. A **spreadsheet** can be either a sheet of paper, marked with a grid, in which financial data is recorded and totals calculated manually or a computer application of such a system, with totals and other formulas figured automatically.

You can use simple spreadsheets on a computer program such as Excel to track your budget. Another option is money management software like Quicken (the most popular), Microsoft Money, You Need a Budget, NeoBudget and Easy Envelope Budget Aid, to name a few. You can also create a spreadsheet using the authors' own online budgeting tool at www.LessonsToMyChildren.com.

In choosing a budgeting program to set up your budget look for the following:

- Easy to set up
- Easy to maintain

- Secure

- Easy to import data say from your bank or credit card account transactions so you can avoid putting in the numbers manually

- Produces reports

- Allows you to tailor it to your personal preferences

- Provides an equally easy way to produce a balance sheet and net worth statement discussed later in this lesson.

Using the software, you can then begin setting up your budget by determining your **total monthly spendable revenue**. Start with your monthly take-home pay, and note what deductions are taken out. Generally these include:

- Tax withholding
- Your share of health insurance offered through your employer
- Your contribution to your 401(k) plan, if offered.

Now, **determine the amount you are obligated to spend each month**: List your fixed monthly recurring expenses such as:

- Rent/mortgage
- Car payment
- Auto insurance
- Health insurance (if not paid through withholding from your paycheck)
- 10 percent savings
- One twelfth of all of your **annually recurring obligations**, expenses that generally pop up once or twice per year, but not every month. This would include income tax payments (if not enough is withheld from your pay), annual life insurance premiums and so forth. Add them up, divide them by 12 and set the money aside so you have it when the bills come due.

Next, list your **variable monthly expenses**, costs that may be different amounts each month. Here you will need to estimate and average. These include things like:

- Groceries
- Gas

- Utilities like water, electric, phone, etc.
- Clothing you need.

Here's where you'll need to figure out your discretionary vs. nondiscretionary income. **Discretionary income** is the amount left for spending, investing or saving after taxes and personal necessities (like food, shelter, and clothing) have been paid. Discretionary income includes money spent on luxury items, vacations and nonessential goods and services.

Presumably, there is still some money for discretionary expenses at this point, and you can start budgeting for things such as:

- Vacations
- Toys (things you want but do not need, like the latest flat-screen TV or a Blu-ray player)
- Holiday and birthday gifts
- Dining out and entertainment
- Clothing you want
- Big items you are saving up for, such as a down payment on your next house.

What If You Come Up Short?

If your outgoing expenses are larger than incoming money, then you have a **deficit** in your budget and will need to figure out how to reduce expenses. This can be done in several ways.

- Cut costs through canceling what you do not use or need, such as extra telephone and cable services or dry cleaning expenses

- Brown bag it for lunch
- Reduce dining out
- Buy in bulk
- Comparison shop for cheaper services
- Lower utility bills by turning off lights and using less heating/air conditioning
- Cut down on magazine and internet service subscriptions
- Use mass transit or bicycle
- Avoid ATM fees by banking at your home bank
- Stay away from high-interest credit cards and be aware of any increase in the interest rate of your present credit cards
- Use coupons and discounts and watch for sales on items that you need.

Your goal is to pare down expenses so you can live within your means and have at least 10 percent left to put into a 401K retirement plan or a savings account.

Monitoring and Maintaining Your Budget

Live with and fine-tune your budget for a few months before you firm it up. It can take as much as a year for you to find (or remember) all the expenses you really have.

Most people check their budgets once a month, since statements usually come on a monthly basis. That way you can reconcile your accounts and check your budget at the same time. Even easier, some budget software downloads credit, debt and bank transactions and can reconcile expenditures with your budget.

Software with clear messages attached to a negative cash flow (the bucket tips over) or positive cash flow (dollar signs) can help make the sometimes difficult task of balancing your budget less complicated and frustrating. Regardless of how you maintain your budget, make sure to keep track of how much you spend and how it balances out with your income.

Update your budget whenever there are major changes. You could get a promotion or lose a job, get married, or have a child. Or you finished paying off your car or refinanced your mortgage. These types of situations can have both positive and negative effects on your budget and cash flow and you'll need to sit down and review your total monthly spendable revenue, the amount you are obligated to spend each month (including 1/12 of all annual obligations) and variable monthly expenses. Chances are you'll most likely feel the effects (both positive and negative) on discretionary income, what you have left over after all necessities have been paid.

Tips for Keeping on Track

Create separate bank accounts for separate purposes. For example, you can have the following accounts:

- A rainy day emergency fund
- A pay-the-taxes account
- A business account
- A personal spending account

- Spouse's personal spending account.
- A household expense account.

This works equally well with envelopes. When Mark's mother first married she kept a budget by putting cash in envelopes to cover their expenses. On payday she would take the cash and put the needed amounts in envelopes labeled "rent," "groceries," "gas," "electric bill" and so on. She knew that she could only spend the money in that envelope for that purpose. Her parents did the same thing only they used coins in Mason jars (and they did not have electric, water, or phone bills). Budgeting has been around for a long time!

Keep it simple. You can go overboard when you start and find it impossible to track every single penny that you spend. Instead, stick with simple, broad categories. For example, use "Entertainment" to include movies, theater, shows, sports events, and anything else that fits.

Beware of "wants" that look like "needs." If you cannot make your ends meet, pare down some things that are really "wants" rather than "needs." The box "What If You Come Up Short" in this Lesson provides some specific suggestions.

Make sure your steady income can keep you current with your expenses. You might be expecting a bonus, commission, tax refund, or other extra cash, but these types of windfalls can be unpredictable and may be less than expected or may come much later than anticipated.

Watch for spending creep (inflation). Hold off on spending on your "wants" even after you do get a bonus, raise, tax refund, gift, and so on. You want to make sure you are keeping ahead of inflation. Your expenses will go up too!

It is easier to track credit card purchases than checks. Credit/debit purchases download automatically to budgeting software like Quicken and Microsoft Money and are automatically assigned a budget category. Checks can take weeks to clear and you can get a nasty surprise in your bank balance, if you have forgotten to record one.

Emergency! Or Not?

Sometimes unexpected things happen that can break your budget. Say your car becomes inoperable, you take it to the shop, and the mechanic tells you it will cost $2,000 to repair. Your first impulse might be just to write the check and get it over with. However, stop for a moment and think about the situation to get the big picture. Ask yourself the following:

- What is the source of the emergency? (Normal wear and tear or an accident?)

- Could it have been planned for? (If an accident, how much of the bill will the insurance cover?)

- What caused it?

- Will it recur? (Will this be a one-time repair for as good as new or is it a symptom of an ailing car?)

- How can I avoid or eliminate it going forward? (Would purchasing a new or late model used vehicle be more cost-effective in the long run?)

- What have I learned from the experience? (Getting a second opinion from another mechanic is always a good idea or maybe the dealership where you bought the car might come up with a cheaper solution.)

- Can my rainy day (emergency) fund cover it?

Your **rainy day or emergency fund** should be sufficient to sustain you for up to six months. Avoid borrowing from a credit card or a third-party lender (such as a payday loan company) to cover the emergency. Cut other expenses, forego other pleasures rather than go into debt wherever possible. Debt comes with new expenses such as high interest.

As discussed elsewhere in this book, you start your savings plan by putting away six months of living expenses. If an emergency arises that you have not budgeted for, use some of this money. However, be sure to replace it before continuing with your other savings goals.

A Net Worth Statement – The Big Picture

In addition to making and having a budget, you'll also need to create a **net worth statement**, a personal balance sheet of your **assets** (what you own) and **liabilities** (what you owe). Taken together, the net worth statement and budget can provide an overall snapshot of your financial health. When making up a net worth statement, first you list everything you own and total it up.

Total value of all Assets (current values)

- House
- Other real estate
- Vehicles, boats and airplanes
- Savings
- Checking
- Investments
- Retirements accounts

- Insurance
- Personal effects
- Collectibles
- Miscellaneous

Then you list everything you owe and total it up.
Total Liabilities (current values)

- Mortgages
- Equity lines of credit
- Car loans
- Education loans
- Credit cards
- Business loans
- Other

Subtract total assets from total liabilities and you will have your net worth. In other words, your **net worth** is the difference between assets and debts. Smart investors try to increase their net worth by acquiring more assets and by reducing debts. See the book's Web site for a useful balance sheet tool.

You can review your net worth monthly, quarterly or annually. Over time, the net worth statement can provide a quick and easy reference as to whether your net worth is increasing or decreasing. You can assess where you are in your financial situation; and it can provide a blueprint for future investment strategies.

TIP FOR THE PARENT: Once upon a time, I remember seeing a young mother at the supermarket with her pre-school aged boy. They were walking down the aisle when the little boy saw a toy that he wanted his mom to buy for him. "Mommy! Mommy! Look, I want that!" he said. She said "Okay, honey," reached into her purse, and pulled out a little note pad. She wrote down the name of the store and the name of the toy, at the foot of what was her little boy's wish list. "Now at the end of the month, we'll take out this list and you'll get to pick one for us to buy." No doubt, every item on that list was something that the little boy had been terribly excited about. I can't help but wonder how many of these items he even remembered when the end of the month came. A child's mind is like a sponge at an early age. They learn from everything they observe and do. The sooner they understand the value of savings and deferred gratification the better it will be ingrained in them.

Take This to the Bank

- Gather the data from pay slips, checkbooks, credit- and debit-card statements, tax returns, and investment accounts for your budget.

- Find software that matches your skills and aptitude in putting together a budget.

- Figure out the links to the various financial accounts that you can download and easily put into your budget spreadsheet or software.

- Write out a budget and track it on a weekly or monthly basis.

- Think twice before you use a credit card. Make sure you can pay it off by the end of the month or before interest starts accruing.

- Use the money-saving tips suggested in this Lesson to add to your available cash.

- Bone up on your math to make sure you can apply it to your budget in everyday life.

- In addition to the budget, a net worth statement is important in providing an overall picture of your financial health, and is essential to planning your future.

Parting Shot

Every dollar bill represents an opportunity to spend it, gift it, save and invest it, buy insurance with it to cover risk, or use it to pay taxes. The wise strategist allocates each dollar and then knows where it goes and how and when it will be used. A budget is the smart way to move forward and avoid financial pitfalls from emergencies and living from paycheck to paycheck.

But a budget alone is not enough. It must have a positive cash flow and must be accompanied by a net worth statement, so you can track your upward progress and avoid any downward spiral.

LESSONS TO MY CHILDREN

Have a Game Plan

He who fails to plan, plans to fail.

Proverb

Setting financial goals is a smart choice and can be very rewarding. When you set a financial goal, you define what you want and develop a plan for achieving it. Instead of wandering aimlessly, you decide where you are going, how you are going get there and when you plan on arriving. You have something to strive for.

Setting a financial goal is just like setting a personal goal. If you want to buy a car, you must come up with a plan for paying for it. This might mean having to make some trade-offs. You decide where to cut back expenses, how much money you'll need to save each month, and how long it will take you to save up for a down payment. A mental picture of yourself in your new ride will provide motivation to stick to your plan.

A Game Plan Starts With a Goal

Erin's Story

Before I went off to college, Dad asked me to outline a five-year plan that included the lists of classes I planned to take as well as degrees I planned to obtain. He also wanted me to figure out where I wanted to live and work after I graduated.

At first I thought this was a pain, but then Dad told me a story about his grandparents. In the 1930s, during the Great Depression, they decided to build a summer cottage on a lake in New Hampshire. It was to be used by their two sons including Dad's father (my grandfather) and their future families. My grandfather owned it after them and he and his brother brought Dad and all the other kids up to summer there.

It's still in our family today. Every summer, the clan gets together and I get to see my cousins, uncles, and grandparents. Now they're making plans to transition it to us, the fourth generation, so we too can enjoy it with our children. However, maintaining the cottage requires a great deal of planning, organization, and shared responsibilities.

In the 1950s, my great-grandparents set up a trust to maximize the inheritance and minimize the taxes and related expenses. They did annual gifting and with appreciation in values they managed to move what totaled over $10M to their descendants without estate taxes. They also made provisions for the cottage in their wills, and after they passed away, the family organized a limited partnership. The message was not lost on their adult children who fostered the same values in their own estate planning and even us, their college–age children.

My family's meticulous planning helped as the older generation lost capacity and became ill. The children were able to take care of things efficiently and effectively due to the legal documents that empowered them to step in. So while figuring this stuff out is a lot of work, it makes sense, especially when you're protecting your money, property, and future.

How Do I Set a Goal?

Actually, setting a goal can be pretty simple. What do you love to do? Chances are it is easy for you and you are pretty good at it. Do you absolutely love music? Are you playing your guitar all the time? Perhaps a career in music will satisfy your needs. If so, make plans to grow, be happy, and make a positive contribution in this arena.

Realize, however, that very few serious musicians make it to the big time, and even fewer accumulate lasting wealth. That generalization applies across the entertainment industry, from actors to TV personalities to comedians and professional athletes. So if you want this kind of life, be prepared to live frugally, save as much as you can, and have a good backup plan.

Any vocation that depends upon your ability to perform physically, such as being an athlete, places you one accident away from the end of your career. Because this type of job is so vulnerable – and your peak years in it may be limited anyway – you'll need a backup plan. A dancer might turn to choreography and a football player or other athlete might become a coach in his or her field. For example, a young ballerina friend of Mark's became disillusioned after dancing professionally for two years. She now is back in college studying to be a doctor and is interested in specializing in sports medicine. In addition to doing ballet at least four hours a day while in high school, she maintained very good grades and her parents made sure they had enough money saved for her college.

If what you're doing now is not supporting your larger goals then it may be time to make a change. Figure out what you really want and map out a transition that will get you from where you are now to where you want to be.

Goal Setting 101

The first thing to do is sit down and make a list of your goals. Writing something down makes it real and also allows you think it over, revise it, and define it even more. Share your goals with family or friends. They will provide support and encouragement, and may offer ideas to help you achieve the goal more effectively and sooner. They can also help you celebrate each step along the way.

You might want to think about setting goals for various aspects of your life. These include categories that you use over time including:

- Education
- Professional growth
- Personal growth
- Personal health
- Immediate family
- Extended family and friends

- Leisure (entertainment, vacations, etc.)
- Financial
- Investments
- Savings
- Risk management (insurance)
- Retirement
- Anything else you can think of.

Once you have determined your larger goal and the general path you will be taking, you can work on specifics. Say you are fascinated by other cultures and peoples and have decided to be a cultural anthropologist. You learn that all the interesting, well-paying jobs in that field require a PhD in anthropology and proficiency in at least one other language. So right away a goal would be to get your PhD and language skills. You will also be traveling the world for much of your career, so if you also want to be married and raise a family, your spouse will need to move around with you. So another goal would be to look for a potential partner who shares your passion for travel and has the type of job – such as a teacher, writer or software engineer – that enables him or her to be mobile.

Your work as an anthropologist may be at a large institution like the Smithsonian with a well-developed health, retirement, and benefits plan. Or you may be with a very small company that lives from one research grant to the next, in which case you are probably on your own for these types of benefits. Until you have the career job, however, you cannot plan beyond the "you are hired" letter.

Use Backwards Planning

One of the more effective strategies in goal-setting is **backwards planning**. That is, identify your ideal goal and/ or where you want to end up and then work backwards from there to the present using a series of logical steps. Start by asking yourself what you want to do in life; where you want to live; who you want to be around; and what will make you safe, happy, and challenged. Then work your way back to the present by figuring out the steps needed to reach that goal.

For example, say you have debt because of student loans. So you decide to become debt-free within three years of graduating from college. Once you have determined the end result, figure out how much you will have to pay a month to get out of debt. Consider the fact that the starting salary of any job that you take will no doubt include pay increases, so you may not need to make such large payments for the first year or so. You can also factor in how much paying off the student loans will affect your budget when you purchase or lease housing, a car, furniture and so forth.

Backwards planning can work for all goals, large or small, planned or unexpected. If you fall in love and decide to get married, you set a date and budget for the wedding. What follows is a backwards plan for one seemingly simple aspect of such an event – getting the invitations out.

Start with the wedding date, in this example it is on May 30th. The invitations should be received six weeks to two months in advance, and figure they will be in the mail for a week before they arrive. So they should be mailed out by the third week in March. It takes a week to label, stuff, seal, and stamp them, so they need be printed and delivered by March 15. All invitees' names and addresses should be squared away by then as well. It takes 3-4 weeks to print the invitations, so your final design should be at the printers by February 15, just to be safe. You need two weeks to come up with and get agreement on the invitation design so start that process by early February at the latest. You should also be working on the list of attendees during that month. That means the budget should be established by mid-January so you know how many people to invite.

Wedding date	May 30
Invitations received two months in advance, mailed out by	March 21
Label, stuff, seal, and stamp invitations – takes about a week, need to receive materials from printer by	March 15
Invitations being printed – 3-4 weeks, so design to printers by	February 15
Final list of invitees – determines number of invites to print, by	February 15
Design and get agreement on invitations. Find for printer – two weeks, by	February 1
Establish budget – sets cost of materials, printing and number of attendees – takes two weeks, start by	January 15

Chart 4.1 Planning Example

Backward planning a career. If you have not yet started your career, learn about what you'll need to reach that goal, and backwards plan from there. For example, if you want to practice law (see following chart), you'll need to pass the bar in the state where you wish to live. To sit for the bar exam you'll need to graduate from law school and should also take a bar exam prep course. To get into law school, you'll need to do well on the Law

School Admission Test (LSAT) and have a bachelor's degree from an accredited college. A variety of Bachelor of Science (BS) or Bachelors of Arts (BA) courses of study are acceptable, although many pre-law students major in English, history, or political science. You need to apply to law schools early in your senior year, so figure out the ones you want to go to and get your applications in before their deadline. To do well on the LSAT you should take it as late in your undergraduate career as possible, preferably at the end of your junior year. You should also take an LSAT prep course right before the exam.

You will have to pay for all of this as well. In addition to your basic living expenses you will need to pay for four years of undergraduate school, an LSAT prep course, the LSAT exam, applications to several law schools, three years of law school, a bar exam prep course, and the bar exam.

Pass bar exam	July 2017
Take bar review course	May-June 2017
Graduate law school	May 2017
Receive bachelors degree	May 2014
Start law school admission process	Fall 2013
Take LSAT	Spring 2013
Take LSAT review course	Winter 2013
Start undergraduate school	Summer 2010
Start undergraduate admissions process	Fall 2009

Chart 4.2 Long-range Planning Example

Backward planning for retirement. Yet another example of backwards planning is retirement. If the goal is a comfortable retirement starting at age 70, the first step is to determine what constitutes a comfortable retirement. Most people can retire on two-thirds of their working salary, because the house should be paid off and the children on their own by then. Because the goal is so many years away, remember to include the time value of money covered in Lesson 2. Let's say you can retire comfortably on $200,000 per year in 40 years. But you expect to collect $50,000 in Social Security and other pensions by then so you'll need to come up with the additional $150,000 per year in 40 years. Play with the retirement calculator found on this book's Web site and you will find different ways to save to the lump sum that will generate the $150,000 and grow to counter inflation. Now that you have your savings figured out, use the budget process from Lesson 3 to figure out your lifestyle expenses with the funds you have left over after saving for retirement.

Tips on Successful Planning

- Put all your plans in writing. Writing something down makes it real and tangible.

- Break the plan down into steps that must be accomplished by a certain date.

- Identify all "must do" items and don't be distracted by the "should do" and the "it would be nice to do" items.

- Be flexible. You will periodically be making revisions to your plan. Also, if the plan is not working or no longer fits, rework the plan until it does.

- Even the most complex task is accomplished one step at a time. Break big steps into smaller, more manageable actions.

- Establish important milestones and reward yourself for getting there. One young man's goal was to serve in the Navy for four years. After his honorable discharge, he took a two-month trip through the Middle East and Asia as his reward.

- Get help. Identify a mentor or two to guide you as you learn the ropes of your chosen career. Also, get professional help in areas where you might not be as sophisticated. Find a good financial planner if you are challenged in budgeting, investing, and saving. See Lesson 9 for more in this regard.

- Inexpensive, easy-to-use project management software can help with certain kinds of planning such as budgeting (Quicken, Microsoft Money), taxes (Turbo Tax) and finances (Quicken, Microsoft Money).

Steps for Successful Planning

Identify and write down all your goals

It could be anything from saving for a new computer or college, a down payment on a condo or a car, or planning for a vacation or retirement. Obviously some goals will take longer to achieve than others, so you need to decide how to best position your money to support your goal. If it's in the short-term, perhaps a 36-month certificate of deposit (CD) or a higher-yield savings account might suffice. If it's for the longer term, see Lesson 8 on investing.

Break big steps into bite-sized segments

Figure how much a month you can reasonably afford and set it aside. If possible, the money should be taken out before you get your paycheck; people don't miss what they can't see.

Flowchart or write out your actions so you can see them

You are more likely to get to the end goal, if you have laid the steps out in front of you.

So when you put your plan on paper, list those steps to be taken tomorrow, two weeks from now, next month, next quarter and so on. This is called a **flow chart**. The flow chart towards the condo/car down payment includes accounts, balances, deposits, and performance benchmarks towards the goal of the desired purchase.

Allow for changes and flexibility

Maybe you find that the drop in the market has affected your investments, so you may need to put in more to meet your goal. Or you might decide to get a smaller condo or a less fancy car, thus reducing the down payment that way.

Plan for tangible results

You will see your portfolio and bank account growing rapidly. This easily measured result can provide a great deal of satisfaction.

Use your game plan to build momentum

If your game plan calls for seven steps and you've completed step five, you can pat yourself on the back for being almost there. You are now excited that this big goal is fast approaching and you redouble your efforts by contributing your work bonus to get there even quicker.

Focus attention on starting and finishing

Life can be full of extraneous demands on your time and energy, making it all too easy to get distracted. Make sure you focus on how you spend your time. If your goal is to save money then close your wallet. If you feel the need to buy something on impulse, take a walk in the woods or visit a friend instead.

This applies to savings and in fact to just about anything else as well. If you want to read three books a quarter for pleasure or professional growth, make sure to set aside a few hours every night or every week to do so.

Get going with a good plan and have a deadline for each step and completion of the plan. Reward yourself every time you finish a step. Set aside adequate time and measure your progress with performance benchmarks. Both are vital to success. It's a good feeling when you take steps in the right direction.

Ask for help and seek advice

While we all hope to learn from our own mistakes, it is much better to learn from another's mistakes. Ask for help and advice whenever you can.

Establish a reward system

When you have success, it's important to reward yourself in a meaningful way. Celebrate each milestone you attain with something special. The reward is obvious when you are saving for a purchase. You can now put the down payment towards the desired item.

Now that you've reached a goal, adapt, revise, and add to your game plan

When you are done saving towards one goal, start another. Now that you have acquired the car you can start putting money towards a new acquisition goal, like a condo. Or you may decide to invest it in stocks, bonds, and securities and increase your overall net worth.

Revisit goals periodically

Anything that involves the future is by its very nature uncertain. You'll need to revisit your goals periodically to adapt and adjust your plan. So, for example, rather than having New Year's resolutions – which are rarely kept anyway – re-evaluate and revise your goals each December. Or you can evaluate them more frequently; say, quarterly or every six months. The point is, you're keeping on top of any changes that need to be made and preventing yourself from getting distracted or losing track of your goals.

At the same time, just because something gets hard does not mean you should immediately throw up your hands in defeat and move on to something else. Nothing worthwhile ever comes without effort. Perseverance (also known as hanging in there) can pay off big. If it was easy, everyone would be doing it.

TIP FOR THE PARENT: When I first went off to college, I had five years of college saved up. I wanted to be a music major, but, upon entering the program, I discovered it would take all five just to get a bachelor's degree and the music department was, in a word, boring. But in talking to my teachers and advisors, I discovered something I did like – English. So I switched majors and will complete the program in the same five years, but with both a bachelor's and a master's degree for the kind of work I love. I simply adjusted my goals to fit my experiences.

Take This to the Bank

- No plan is real until it's written down on paper. That way you know exactly what you need to do.

- Ask yourself how to get there and start the process of figuring out exactly what it will take.

- Also write down who you want to be and where you want to go in life. This will also provide affirmation for your goals and make them more real.

- The earlier you start, the more you will be rewarded. As mentioned before – and especially when it comes to saving money – the early bird catches the worm.

- Take action now. Procrastination is a lose-lose proposition. Nothing gets done and guilt and angst are the only rewards. And especially when dealing with debt, it only gets worse as interest and added fees mount.

- Frequently review and revise your plan. Things change rapidly in this information-based world so it's important to be adaptable and flexible.

- Ask for help. Knowledge is power. And there's no such thing as a stupid question or an unnecessary request for assistance.

- Realize that, although unexpected things do happen, much of your fate lies in your own hands. You simply have to seize the reins and take charge of our future.

Parting Shot

Without a plan, life can be a random journey filled with bad decisions and unnecessary distractions. A plan gives your actions purpose and sets you on the path to success. Sometimes you can get lucky and things work out exactly the way that you want. While that may be cause for gratitude and happiness, when you accomplish what you set out to do, the taste of your rewards is even sweeter because your efforts have resulted in positive outcomes. And it's much easier to navigate rocky waters with a compass and a chart. Plans and goals will keep you on course.

LESSONS TO MY CHILDREN

LESSON 5

Limit Your Debt

*Be assured it gives much more pain to the mind to be
in debt, than to do without any article whatever which
we may seem to want.*

Thomas Jefferson, in a letter to his daughter.

It's all too easy to get caught up in a consumer society and advertisements that make us feel "less than," if we don't purchase their product or service. These companies are all too happy to have us to spend more than we earn as long as we can make the minimum monthly payments.

Debt is a drag on your present and future. Along with robbing you of the time value of money, it steals from your disposable income and savings. However, in some cases debt is necessary, such as when you take out a loan to further your education or purchase a house or your first car. But debt must be manageable at all times. That is, your total combined debt (student loans, house, car, and so forth), should not exceed 35 percent of your **monthly gross income** – what you get from your check before taxes, Social Security, and other deductions are taken out. Generally, your house payment (mortgage, insurance, and property taxes) should not exceed 25 percent of your monthly gross income, so your car expenses should not exceed 10 percent. If you are already in debt beyond these amounts/percentages, then your first priority should be to get your debt under control and down to less than 35 percent.

Definitions, Types, and Categories of Debt

Simply put, **debt** is when you owe something, typically money, to another. When the amounts you owe exceed your assets, you are insolvent. When you are unable to pay your debts, bills, and other obligations as they come due, you are bankrupt. Properly managing your debt and having a good credit rating is critical to your personal, financial, and investment success. A **credit rating** is an estimate, based on previous dealings, of a person's or an organization's ability to fulfill their financial commitments and will be covered later in this Lesson.

There are many terms associated with debt. For example, say Jim asks Susan to lend him $1,500. Susan says OK, but she wants the loan to be in writing and wants $1,600 back in six months. Jim, the borrower, is known as the **debtor**, and Susan as the lender is the **creditor**. The writing evidencing the loan is called a **note**, the **term** is six months and the **interest** is $100. Susan wants the entire balance back plus interest at the term of the note – that is called a **balloon payment**. Because Jim did not have to put up any of his possessions as security to guarantee the loan, the note is **unsecured**.

Debt can be categorized in several ways:

Personal vs. Investment. *Personal debt* is borrowing incurred to support your personal lifestyle choices. That would include your car loan, home mortgage, credit card balance, and so on. *Investment debt* is borrowing related to investments such as a margin account (an account with a brokerage in which the broker extends credit to the owner of the account) or the mortgage on a rental property you own.

Secured vs. Unsecured. Lenders often want more than your promise to pay back the loan. They want you to pledge something of value. For example, when you borrow money to buy a car, the lender will hold title to the car as *security* until the loan is paid off. If you default on the loan, the lender can repossess the car and sell it to recover some of the funds owed. As mentioned in the previous example, loans in which you do not have to put up any possessions are *unsecured.*

Recourse vs. Non-recourse. If in the above car loan example, the proceeds from the sale of the repossessed car are not enough to pay off the loan, the lender can come after the borrower for the deficiency or difference remaining due. This kind of loan is therefore a *recourse* loan, meaning the lender has the recourse to go after the borrower's personal assets. If the lender had no choice but to accept the car as full satisfaction of the loan, it would then be known as a *non-recourse loan.* Virtually all personal secured loans are with recourse. Many investment-related loans, however, are non-recourse.

Revolving Line of Credit. A *revolving line of credit* consists of a loan agreement in which a certain amount of money is able to be borrowed. As long as the loan is repaid, the borrower may obtain more money up to the limit of the agreement without having to apply for a new loan. Home equity lines of credit and credit cards are revolving lines of credit.

Tax-favored vs. Non Tax-favored. Most personal expenses are not tax deductible. One big exception is mortgage interest on your house. It makes home ownership very attractive. If you are paying 6 percent interest on your home mortgage and you are in the 30 percent income tax bracket, your net after tax interest is only 4.2 percent. In a simple example, say you are borrowing $100,000 at six percent on a 30-year home mortgage, your interest is $6,000 in the first year, but you can deduct $6,000 from your income for tax purposes so your tax savings is 30 percent of $6,000 or $1,800. Because you are saving $1,800 in taxes, your actual interest cost is 6,000 less 1,800 or $4,200, which translates into 4.2 percent interest on $100,000.

Compounded Interest vs. Simple Interest. *Compounded interest* is charged on both principal and accumulated interest from prior periods. Virtually all loans in the commercial setting are compound interest. For example, say you borrow $100,000 at a 6 percent annual rate which is compounded monthly. That means that ½ percent of the principal (6 percent divided by 12) is added to your balance each month. If you did not make any payments, your balance at the end of the first month is $100,500, in the second month you add ½ percent of 100,500 and your new balance is $101,002. In the third month your new balance is $101,507.51. By the end of the year your balance is $106,167.78. Monthly compounding added $167.78 additional interest to your loan. Another classic example of compounded interest is taking a penny and doubling it every day for 30 days. If you could get someone to start with a penny and pay you 100 percent interest compounded daily for 30 days, you would have $10.7 million! *Simple interest* is where the interest is a percentage of the principal only. In the above admittedly extreme example, if the bank were to pay 100 percent simple interest every day you would end up with 31 cents.

Contributors to Debt

The biggest contributor to debt is **lack of financial discipline.** Too often purchases are driven by desire rather than a sensible evaluation of your finances. Or you may just "pay as you go" with bills, which can be a slipshod way of managing finances. Not only does an unorganized payment plan prevent you from saving for the future, but it also provides little if any protection against unexpected or catastrophic expenses. And then there is the greatest of all evils, impulse buying, which can be a big-time contributor to debt. Yes, that great pair of shoes or flat screen TV is 50 percent off, but can you really afford it?

The underlying cause of debt can be boiled down to one thing: Living beyond your paycheck. If you are spending more than you are earning, you are incurring debt. Borrowing to pay your current expenses will only make things worse by increasing both expenses and the interest resulting from the borrowed money.

There are only two ways to cure the problem – reduce your expenses or get a better paying job. To reduce your expenses, try going on a spending diet. Resolve to buy only things you really need and nothing else for one month. So, no $5 cups of coffee, no eating out, no movies, and absolutely no impulse buys. You will discover after that month that you really can manage on less and actually save some money in the process. That would be a good time to establish and stick with a budget.

Housing and Mortgages

As mentioned earlier, some debt is necessary and can work to your advantage. Under the right circumstances, buying a house ranks right up there as a smart financial decision. However, you need to know what you're getting into and what the terms will be.

The first step is to qualify for a mortgage. Doing so will tell you how much you can afford to pay for a house. To start this process, you'll need to have your own financial house in order with a budget, a savings plan, a balance sheet, and the ability to manage your debt and credit score. You will also generally need to show two years of steady employment. A lender will look hard at three things: your ability to pay (income); your willingness to pay (credit score); and the collateral (the house).

Lenders generally say that housing expenses should not exceed 25-28 percent of the homeowner's gross monthly income. The housing expenses include monthly mortgage principal, interest payments, property taxes and homeowner's insurance. For Federal Housing Administration (FHA) loans, this figure is not to exceed 29 percent of the homebuyer's gross monthly income. According to the American Housing Survey data, the median annual taxes per $1,000 value averages $12. The median property insurance costs averages $30 per month.

However, to be really safe, try reducing the percentage of income-to-housing costs rate to 25 percent or lower. You can also pay down the balance more rapidly and thus save interest costs by taking out a fifteen-year mortgage or paying extra each month beyond the actual balance due.

So how do you calculate your income-to-mortgage percentage? Generally you count:

- Wages and commissions

- Self-employment income

- Social security or retirement income

- Alimony and child support

- Worker's compensation

- Investment income

- Trust or other income

Lenders also want to know not only how much income you make, but how reliable it is. If your income is variable and consists of bonuses and commissions, lenders are going to want to see evidence that it does come at regular, dependable intervals. You will also need to show the lender your employment history, your balance sheet showing all your assets and liabilities, and your income tax returns. The lender will obtain your credit score and will need to see an appraisal of the property you are purchasing before they agree to lend you the funds.

Another important aspect of mortgages is **underwriting**, a process in which a large financial service provider, such as a bank or insurer, assesses the eligibility of a customer to receive a product such as a mortgage or a loan. And while many institutions do have the money to lend you to buy your house, many loans today are actually underwritten by private investors or by Fannie Mae or Freddy Mac – federal agencies whose purpose is to make funds available for home mortgages. These investors and agencies may have additional requirements.

Car Loans

Buying a car can be a tough decision. Do you want to pay cash for an old clunker that will cost you in terms of constant repairs and time lost during breakdowns? Or should you purchase a newer or more reliable car, even though it will lose value the moment you drive it off the lot? Or do you need a car at all?

If you live in a major city like New York, Chicago, or San Francisco which has excellent public transportation, the answer to the last question is "no" and you can skip over this section. However, for any place else you'll likely need a reliable car to keep a job and live independently. Before you start shopping for your car, you need to establish your budget, both in terms of the price of the car and also your monthly payment schedule. Let's say your budget is $20,000 for the price of the car, and you have saved up $2,000 in cash. Most lenders want you to put some of your own funds into the vehicle and will lend only up to 80-90 percent of the value of the car. You need to come up with the remainder in cash and this part is called the **down payment**.

Remember that your car payment should not exceed 10 percent of your monthly income. Your gross income is $52,000 per year, ($4,333 per month) so your monthly payment should be no more than $433. So, you need to borrow $18,000 and you would like to pay it off in three years. You also will pay about $40 in fees and 6 percent in sales tax, both of which you will finance. The prevailing interest rate for this kind of loan is 4 percent, so using the loan calculator such as the one at this book's Web site, you will find that your monthly payment is $568.04. This is more than your budget. You can either find a cheaper car or extend the term of the loan. If you are going for the cheaper car, the most car you can buy with a 3-year, 4 percent interest (plus fees and tax) is $15,685. You have fallen in love with the $20,000 car, however, so if you extend the term of the loan to 48 months your monthly payment becomes $434.42, close enough! The purchase price of the car is $21,240 ($40 in fees and $1,200 in sales tax). You are financing $19,240. Your payments add up to $20,449.44 after 4 years. That plus your $2,000 down payment makes the cost of your car $22,449.44, of which $1,209.44 is interest.

Recurring Charges

Examine your expenses closely for **recurring charges**. These are fees you pay every month for a product or service, such as for auto insurance or utilities. However, some recurring charges may be unnecessary. Are you really reading that magazine? Are you actually using the health club enough to justify the expense? Sometimes it is better to just pay as you go rather than have a subscription or just buy a few weights and exercise outside. Even purchasing an expensive piece of gym equipment such as a treadmill that you use constantly may be more cost-effective in the long run.

Recurring charges can add up. Say, for instance, you agree to a "free" service for three months such as identity theft protection but forgot to call back and cancel the service after the trial was up. It may have only been for a minimal amount; say $10 a month, but that adds up to $120 over the course of the year. Even something as small as paying $5 a month insurance on a cell phone – especially when there's a $50 deductible and it only covers issues like certain technical malfunctions and not dropping or losing it – should be closely examined. Do you really need to pay $60 a year when a replacement can be purchased on eBay or at a discount store for under $100? Small matters make a difference and add up.

Credit Cards

We've said it before, credit cards make it all too easy to spend money you don't have. An effective strategy for someone with a persistent credit card balance would be to pay it off and never use the cards again. You can switch to debit cards and keep a sharp eye on your bank account balances to avoid overdrawing on the account itself.

A good rule of thumb when using credit cards: Make sure you have enough in the checking account to pay the bill when it comes due. If you can stick with this habit, then you can use the cards to your benefit, taking advantage of sales that provide discounts and percentages off. However, more often than not the credit card companies are betting that you *won't* have the funds to pay them off in full and they can stick you with high interest and fees if you fail to pay off the balance.

Just look at the figures. According to the Nilson Report on consumer spending, in 2008, there were 26.5 billion credit card transactions totaling $2.1 trillion. That's up from 21 billion transactions totaling $1.4 trillion in 2003. At the end of 2008, Americans' credit card debt reached $972.73 billion, up 1.12 percent from 2007. The average outstanding credit card debt for households with a credit card was $10,679 at the end of 2008.

So if you're just starting out in this game, use debit cards. This will prevent you from spending money you do not have and will help you will live within your means, rather than getting into debt over your head.

Understanding Credit Scores

Lenders have two primary concerns when they are evaluating

you as a candidate for a loan: return *of* their money and return *on* their money. To evaluate your ability to pay them back, they are going to collect a lot of information about you. This will include your income and expenses, your job stability, your personal assets, and, perhaps most importantly, your credit score/rating.

The most common credit score is known as the FICO score, a mathematical model developed by Fair, Isaac Corporation (hence the initials FICO). It applies to all borrowers the same way, regardless of income, gender, race, religion, address, and so on. The three credit reporting agencies, Experian, TransUnion and Equifax, rate borrowers on their ability to pay and assign them FICO credit scores.

If you have ever borrowed money (outside of family and friends) you have a credit score. You should pay attention to your score and always try to keep it as high as possible. The highest possible score is 850. Having a good credit score (680 is considered good, 760 or higher is best) means lenders are more willing to lend and can offer you better terms. It will save you a lot of money. For example, if you were borrowing $200,000 for a 30-year fixed-rate single family home mortgage, here are the interest rate differences as of this writing:

Credit Score	APR	Monthly Payment	Total Interest Paid
760-850	4.61%	$1,026	$169,534
700-759	4.832%	$1,053	$179,153
680-699	5.009%	$1,075	$186,908
660-679	5.223%	$1,101	$196,383
640-659	5.653%	$1,155	$215,746
620-639	6.199%	$1,225	$240,931

Chart 5.1 Credit Scores and their effect on borrowing

The lower the score the greater the interest and the higher the monthly payment. In fact, the homeowner with the lowest credit score pays over *$70,000 more in interest* over the life of the mortgage!

How credit scores are calculated

About one-third of your credit report is based on your payment history. This includes all your current and historic accounts (credit cards, installment agreements, retail credit accounts, finance company accounts, mortgages, etc.) as well as any adverse public records such as bankruptcies, judgments, law suits, liens, delinquency/past due accounts and collection items. Credit agencies understand that nobody is perfect so they also keep track of how long ago any adverse item happened. If you have adverse items in your past, their effect on your credit score will slowly fade and generally be gone after 7-10 years, assuming you avoid additional adverse items. In other words, late payments will lower your score, but restoring a good payment record will slowly raise your score.

The second-third of the credit score is based on the amount you owe. Credit agencies look at the number and types of accounts with balances, what percentage of your credit limit in an account is borrowed, and what percentage of each loan is still borrowed. If your overall borrowing is low compared to your total available credit limit, and you keep a good cushion between your available credit and your current balance on each debt, you are less likely to overextend yourself financially and this improves your credit score.

The last and final third of the credit score is based upon how long you have had a credit history, applications for new credit (how many, how often, how recent), and the type of credit used.

Make a point of guarding and monitoring your credit at least annually. Get and review your credit report and make sure that any errors are promptly repaired. You are entitled to a free copy of your credit report from each of the three reporting agencies each year. To get your report go to www.annualcreditreport.com. Also preserve a good credit rating by limiting the amount of debt you carry and paying all your bills on time.

Debt Red Flags

Credit card companies and other lenders didn't become a billion-dollar, high-profit industry because they are charities. They use all kinds of tactics to lure you in, such as promising zero interest, no down payment loans. Say you decide to take out such a loan for a car. Look more closely and you may find that the price of the vehicle is much higher than what it would have been had you paid cash or gone through a more conventional form of financing. Zero percent cards can be another trap; they may carry penalties if you pay off the balance before the lower interest rate expires. Such terms are often buried in the small print.

Credit card companies have also preyed on college students, offering credit lines far out of proportion to students' financial means, reaching $10,000 or more for even those without jobs. According to msnbc.com, some unsophisticated students had no idea what their obligations would be. As they built up balances on their cards, they found themselves trapped in a maze of jargon and baffling fees, with annual interest rates shooting up to more than 30 percent.

However, on May 22, 2009, President Barack Obama signed into law the *Credit Card Accountability, Responsibility and*

Disclosure Act of 2009. Under the new law, no one under age 21 can get a credit card unless a parent, guardian or spouse is willing to co-sign or unless the young adult has proof of sufficient income to cover the financial obligations. The law took effect February 2010 and is part of a larger credit card reform effort, including protection against arbitrary interest rate increases, non-penalization of cardholders who pay within the grace period (preventing double-cycle billing which racks up late payment fees) and protection from due date gimmicks and misleading terms, among other things.

What follows are some other things to watch out for when borrowing money:

- *Adjustable Rate Mortgages.* These mortgages entice you with a very low initial interest rate and then will raise it after three, five, or seven years. If you are at the limit of your budget with the lower rate when you take out the loan, how are you going to pay the mortgage when the interest goes up? Because it avoids any increase in your mortgage, a 30-year fixed rate mortgage is a much better deal, even though it may cost more initially and you may have to jump through more hoops to get approval.

- *Prepayment penalties.* Lenders have expenses and need to make a profit. They make their money from the interest you pay. If you pay off the loan too early, they do not make enough interest for the loan to be worthwhile, and it may not even cover their expenses. So in a commercial lending situation with large dollar amounts, lenders typically include a limited pre-payment penalty. For example, a large commercial mortgage might include a two-year prepayment penalty since the lender needs to make at least two-years' worth of interest to make the loan worthwhile. In a consumer setting, however, prepayment penalties are rare. Just to be safe, however, ask questions to make sure that there is no such penalty on your car, home, or any other consumer debt you incur.

• *Rule of 78 loans.* This particularly nasty type loan uses the so-called "Rule of 78" prepayment penalty in which a formula determines accelerated interest. These "pre-computed" loans are still found in several states, especially in the subprime market targeting people with poor credit. You can also spot them if the financing contract talks about refund or rebate of interest. Rule of 78 loans in excess of five years have been banned under Federal law, and all types of these loans are now illegal in 17 states. Obviously they should be avoided at all costs.

How to Get Out and Stay Out of Debt

It's a lot easier to avoid debt in the first place than have to dig out from under a mountain of debt. What follows are some simple tips:

• Keep your expenses down

• Live below your means

• Carry cash

• Only use prepaid credit cards if you must due to travel or other factors that require a credit card.

If you are already in debt, you can take steps to get out of it. The first is by using **discretionary** or **disposable income** which is what is left after you subtract your basic living expenses including housing, utilities, groceries and transportation from your monthly take-home pay and other income. Then compare your disposable income to your debts. Using simple math, or the debt calculator found on this book's Web site, figure out how many months it would take to pay off your short-term debts (e.g., credit cards) realizing that interest payments will increase the actual amount owed. Then set up a plan to apply as much disposable income as possible to those credit card bills.

Also:

- Give each dollar a job such as pay for the rent or mortgage and so on.

- Keep track of your debt.

- After listing your debt in order of highest interest rate first, start paying off the highest rate of debt first without incurring penalties with any other debt. Track your balances month after month. Make a contest of how fast you can reduce the debt.

- Don't make any new purchases until all of the old purchases are paid off.

You might be asked to **co-sign** for a loan. That is, you can sign for another person's debt which legally obligates you to make payments on the loan should that person default. In order to do this, you must have an acceptable credit background and must meet the required amount of income which can vary depending on the bank and the type of loan.

If you ever watch any courtroom TV shows, many of the cases involve inexperienced people who have co-signed loans and other contracts (such as cell-phone services) for friends and significant others. Not surprisingly, when the other party defaulted, they ended up on reality TV with the hopes of resolving the dispute and paying off the bill. So, along with ruining your finances and credit rating by co-signing for someone else, consider whether you'd want to end up like the people on those shows!

If you find yourself thinking about asking a friend or relative to co-sign on a loan for you, be prepared to pay it back in full, under the terms set forth by the loan. If you default on the loan, you may be ruining their credit rating and finances and seriously impairing the relationship. It's best to avoid co-signing altogether; if you don't have the money – or can't borrow it on your own – then forego the purchase.

Additional suggestions

- Limit credit card debt. Only charge what you can pay off in full each month. If you have trouble doing that, cut up the cards and pay for everything with cash or a debit card.

- Pay your bills on time; otherwise you can incur a late charge and hurt your credit rating. With credit cards, the charges are particularly high since you also have to pay interest on the balance for the month.

- Dial-down big events. For example, a wedding is (hopefully) a once-in-a-lifetime event and everyone wants to make it especially memorable. The average cost for a wedding with 150 guests is $20,000, not including the honeymoon and engagement ring. However, if you pare the guest list down to 75, you'll have enough left over for a down payment on your house.

If all else fails

If you think you need personal counseling to manage your debt, start with the National Foundation for Credit Counseling (NFCC). They set the standards for accreditation of **credit counseling** agencies. Find a credit counselor who is accredited by NFCC. Steer clear of any agency that claims they can do such things as removing your debt or getting bad credit off your credit report. Also be wary of those who ask you to pay them and they will pay your bills, or who want to be paid a percentage of the debt they promise to get rid of. Some debt consolidation services are excellent and can help pay off debt in 3-4 years, by using lawyers to negotiate settlements and setting up a trust fund with a 3rd party bank. But check them out first with Better Business Bureau, state consumer protection agencies, and references.

TIP FOR THE PARENT: Don't let a student have a credit card. Start them with only a checking account and, if necessary, a debit card. Avoid co-signing on your children's purchase of a house or a car. That puts you personally at risk and involves you in your children's finances in a way that fosters dependence, not independence. If absolutely necessary gift them the money to help with a down payment but make sure they buy what they can afford not what they can get with your additional help.

Take This to the Bank

- Credit cards are a trap. Only use them if you can afford to pay off the balance each month. They profit from you the most and you lose the most if you carry a balance.

- If you are at the credit limit of your cards all the time, it signals that you are a poor credit risk and it will lower your credit score.

- Avoid debt if at all possible.

- Avoid impulse purchases.

- Keep track of your debt.

- Be frugal – brown bag it for lunch, limit dining out, and look for and use coupons, discounts, and sales on items that you normally need.

- Limit yourself to one or two credit cards.

- Try paying for everything with cash as you would be surprised how much your expenses will drop simply because you have made it harder to spend.

- Trade for services. Mow your neighbor's lawn and have them help you with a repair job that they can do well.

- If you are responsible with your debt and pay all your bills on time, you will build a good credit score, which is necessary to buy a house and helps in getting a good interest rate on the mortgage.

Parting Shot

Smart consumers see the latest bells and whistles touted by advertisements for what they are – a way for someone to make money off of a buyer's insecurities or desire to keep up with the Joneses. If you ignore those signals and purchase only what you need, then you will have much better control over your money, saving it instead of going into debt. However, if you have dug yourself into a credit card black hole, the only way out is to STOP SPENDING. Think about every single purchase and whether or not you actually need it. Make a list of all your expenses and see where your money goes. Simply being aware of how and when you spend will help you think twice before you swipe the card and they swipe your money. Better yet, use cash, checks, or a debit card, keeping track of those expenses as well so you don't overdraw at the bank and you have enough for your monthly expenses and saving needs.

LESSON 6

You Get What You Pay For

There ain't no such thing as a free lunch
(also known as TANSTAAFL)

Most people need money to survive and even more so to thrive. So if you are looking to spend money for something, remember there are two sides to every transaction. A deal where the other side loses will not be in their best interest and if that happens, they may not want to do business with you again. So along with receiving good value for your money or time, make sure the other party benefits as well. That way you will have repeat business and the profits will flow both ways.

Cost vs. Value

"You get what you pay for." This is a very old saying and there is a reason why it has been around for a long time. With rare exceptions, your cost is a good indicator of the value you are receiving. But it is not always easy to determine an item's true cost or value. That is why you should not buy on price alone. Price is one of several factors that make up the cost, and it tells you little about value such as what is the item worth to you?

- *Cost.* Of course the price you are paying is part of the "cost." But what about other hidden costs? How much is your time worth? Your frustration?

Sam's Story

It was time for me to replace my car. I found two models that met my needs: One was very reliable, cost $3,000 more than the other model and only had a 36-month warranty. The other, cheaper and less reliable car had a better 10-year warranty. Because my time is valuable and I needed a car that I could depend on, I went with the first one. The second one might "cost" me much more in terms of frustration from being stuck and having to do repairs. Someone else might reasonably choose to go with the second car because dependability might not be as important as the $3,000 difference in price.

- *What if the item or service is "free?"* "There is no such thing as a free lunch" is an even older saying. In business or commercial settings "free" simply means that your cost is hidden somewhere else.

Generally nothing in a business or commercial setting is truly free. If you are offered something for free, and it's not charity, look closely at what the cost involves and make sure there are no hidden fees. If a person is providing a service to you with no apparent cost, ask for a breakdown of expenses. Their cost or fee will be included as part of that package. They cannot afford to do this for free and survive financially. The goal is not to see if you can deny the service provider that fee. The goal is to figure out what the service provider's incentive or motive is for selling you this product, and whether the actual amount you are paying them is reasonable.

Erin's Story

My family and I were on vacation in Orlando and were offered two free tickets to an amusement park, worth $100 each, if we spent three hours listening to a timeshare pitch. It was the most unpleasant three hours of the entire trip, especially considering that we spent $3,500 for seven vacation days, and had about 35 hours available for activities after subtracting travel, meals, exercise, sleep, and so forth. So when I broke it down dollar-wise, my "vacation time" was worth $100 per hour and their pitch ended up "costing" *me* a total of $100!

- *Value.* Determining overall value is much harder than determining cost. To begin with, it can be difficult to understand what you are getting. A good example is a cell phone service contract or an insurance annuity. What are you actually getting for your money? Are there any hidden fees or service charges? If necessary, get help from a trusted advisor to help you read "the fine print." Second, value is relative. All you really care about is what it is worth to you. Does the item or service completely solve a problem or fill a need, or are there gaps? How long will it continue to meet your needs? The two $100 "free" tickets to the amusement park might be very valuable to you and well worth the high-pressure pitch to buy a timeshare.

Buying On Price Alone

In certain situations, however, it makes sense to use price as the major factor in financial decisions, such as:

- When the same product is sold through many stores

- For interchangeable products where quality is similar

- For low cost, highly competitive services, such as dry cleaning

- When you can only afford to pay the minimum

- Where the seller offers no premium or value over the product itself

You buy the cheapest when the value is identical and the other "costs" are unimportant. This book, for example, is the same whether you purchase it from an online vendor at a discount or from a bookstore. However, you may prefer the intangible "values" of actually going into a bookstore and browsing and enjoying a cup of coffee in the café, and holding the book in your hands before buying. You may also feel that you need to have it right now, even though if you wait, the online vendor will give you a better deal.

Spending vs. Investing

Much of American culture has become rooted in consumerism, which is generally the "spend it now" approach to value, also known as **instant gratification**. The consumer accounts for most of the U.S. economy. Only recently did the U.S. consumers wake up to the realization that they were spending more than they had by running up debt on credit cards or equity lines of credit, which resulted in a negative rate of savings.

Every time you chose to spend a dollar, it is **consumed** or used up. In essence, it pays for today and, for the most part, you receive instant satisfaction or gratification for your expenditure. What you spend it on may be necessary for survival such as food, clothes, housing, and transportation. It may be to support a certain level of quality of life, like eating out or going to a movie. Your dollars can even be used for luxuries, such as a cruise vacation you always dreamed of taking. Your net benefit might be characterized as "taking care of today." You survive and even thrive off of expenditures, but once you spend it, it is gone forever.

However, every dollar you productively invest is a gift that keeps on giving over time since it produces more than what you started with. That is **deferred gratification**, and can be sweeter than the quick spend, since you are accumulating savings and financial security.

Deferred gratification can work in other ways, such as turning down the thermostat in winter (and keeping it higher in summer) to save on energy bills, help the environment, and increase your spending power.

Logic vs. Emotion

When making purchases, logic and emotion both count. The preferred color of a dress or a shirt is a matter of personal taste. Does it complement your outfit? Does your tie go with it? Do your shoes have to match and so on? Still you probably only shop in certain stores due to proximity, price, value, earned reputation or other factors that are both objective and subjective.

Applying logic alone may not be enough, however. For example, Jim researched which car to buy based on criteria such as functional use, independent test results, and price. He found several that fit the bill, and asked his wife to come to the dealership and check them out. As she walked past the row of new cars, she immediately fell in love with one that was completely different from those Jim had chosen. However, the good news was that the price was comparable as was the Consumer Report rating, but it had two doors instead of four. The distinguishing factor (number of doors) was subjective and Jim's wife, and later his daughter drove the vehicle for close to ten years.

However, some decisions require more than a first impression. Jim's cousin Nancy was looking to buy a new home in Colorado. She went through many listings, including one high up the side of a mountain overlooking the valley. Along with being beautifully appointed, it was actually the best value for the money. She initially dismissed it and it quickly sold. But the buyer backed out and she had the opportunity to tour it again. Although she was reticent, she agreed to do so because it was such a good deal. She fell in love with it – her initial hesitation was due to altitude sickness, which she'd since overcome. Had she let her emotion trump her logic, she and her husband would have never gotten their dream house.

When investing money, however, logic needs to prevail. Oftentimes people make purchases emotionally and then use logic and reason to justify their decision. If you do this with investment and finance, then you might as well spend your money on lottery tickets.

The key is – will you allow reason to dissuade you from making an emotional purchase? The marketing and advertising industries bet that you won't. Let's say there is a really cool HD flatscreen TV that you just have to have, but it is not in your budget, and besides, there is nothing wrong with your current TV. To be successful, you need to let logic and reason override emotional buying decisions so you can resist purchasing unnecessary items and services.

Be a Smart Shopper

Smart shoppers get more for their dollar, balancing emotion and logic in purchasing decisions. However, they need to be aware of certain pitfalls.

The first, **credit cards,** have made impulse buyers out of many people. Because you can charge it now and pay much later, the consequences of using the cards are too far removed from the actual purchase. For example, a twelve-month no payment charge for furniture (It's "free" for a year, right?)can easily result in a high interest rate and higher cost; and your $1,500 sofa will be more like $1,900 if you don't pay it in full by the date it's due.

Debit cards and checking accounts can also cause problems for impulse spenders. Ever heard the saying, "How can I be overdrawn? I still have checks left." Unfortunately sometimes people see what they want and do have the money at the time, failing to consider that other bills are due or are automatically withdrawn from their accounts at certain times of the month.

If you have these kinds of issues, then cut up your credit/debit cards, shred the checks and only use cash.

Smart shoppers also use **lists.** Lists can be used for everything from groceries to "to-do" items and can give you a clear idea of how to spend your time and money. There's also a great satisfaction in completing the list – check it off and it's done. Lists also keep you on task and prevent you from forgetting important items. They keep you organized, efficient, and help you avoid doing or buying things you do not really need.

Coupons, sales, and discount stores (such as Costco and Sam's Club) can also help you save money. However, avoid buying things not on your list. It's not a bargain if you don't need it and can't afford it. Purchasing large quantities at a discount can be cost saving for non-perishable items like soaps and paper products if you have the space to store them. Also make sure the bigger price tag on the bulk item fits within your budget.

Be a Smart Investor

Confucius said: Real knowledge is to know the extent of one's ignorance. This is especially true of investing. When you are starting out, the investment world can be confusing and full of traps. Say you hire someone to help you manage your finances. Does the advisor work on a fixed fee or a commission? If they get paid based on commission, what assurance do you have that their advice is good for you or just good for their monthly report? You want advice that's best for you – not them.

If an advisor offers to sell you something or do something for free – absent easy explanations like family relationships or charity – you should probably worry more about them than someone who charges or sells to you at a reasonable price. Why are they giving it away? Where are the hidden fees? And how can someone be in business if they provide their services for nothing?

Worksheet/Checklist

In investing or buying, ask yourself the following:

- What will you receive in return for the investment or purchase in terms of goods, services, or safeguards?

- How much will it cost in direct and indirect money, time, energy, or other costs?

- Are there alternatives, what are they, and what are their respective advantages and disadvantages?

- Does the person or firm you are dealing with appear knowledgeable and trustworthy?

- Regarding any future adversities, are there safeguards or protections such as warranties, checks on investment results, and audits?

TIP FOR THE PARENT: The parents paid allowances based on each child's chores. The youngest remembers that when she was in middle school, her dad gave her an allowance and then went to give her older brother his allowance as well. Her brother turned down the money from her Dad, saying that he hadn't earned the money that week yet. She was totally FLOORED that her brother was turning down free money. Her siblings and she received their allowances every week while growing up, and the allowance increased with the number of chores that they did. That helped her understand the contractual nature of money and also put a premium on saving to get larger items that she desired, which taught her delayed gratification.

Take This to the Bank

- If something sounds too good to be true, it probably is.

- A penny saved is a penny earned – as long as you don't waste it someplace else.

- Don't be afraid to ask for details – there's no such thing as a stupid question, especially if it involves your money.

- Make sure you understand the fee structure before you engage anyone for financial services. Know what you are paying for and beware of "free" services. Oftentimes such costs are hidden and you don't know how much you are paying.

- Win-win equations work best for the long haul. "I bought this cheaper on the Internet than in any store" and yet the person selling it made a profit.

- "I win, you lose," is only good once. "I lost money last time I sold to you and I will not do that again, but I will be happy to make up for my losses this time around for this price."

- When shopping for products, check them out beforehand. Do your homework. Subscribe to Consumer Report-type services to gain additional insights. Buying with purpose, rather than on the spur on the moment, works best.

- When shopping for services check them out as well on the Web, professional licensing organizations, and consumer services organizations. Ask your friends, relatives, or anyone whose judgment you trust for referrals.

Parting Shot

Everything you buy should be carefully evaluated for value. "Deals" or "specials" are marketing tools designed to give one person or firm an advantage over another. Look carefully under the hood, regardless of whether it's a car, a computer, or a financial investment. Something that's really cheap or is an off-brand may break down, costing you more in lost time and repairs.

You want the best buy for your money and sometimes that involves spending more. So carefully weigh the pros and cons of each purchase, do your homework in researching the product or service, and ask for the opinions of those you trust. In a highly competitive market place, oftentimes the distinguishing factor is not the product itself but its **value proposition** – the sum total of tangible and intangible benefits that the client or customer will receive. If you have a one-time transaction, you need not worry about the value to the other side of your transaction. However, if you want to have an ongoing relationship, such as with an investment advisor, it has to work for both parties.

Balance Risk and Reward

Backwards we walk through life, seeing not what lies ahead, but only where we have been

Mark Cohen

Much of life is a balance between risk and reward. Say you are in a hurry and are contemplating going above the speed limit. If you do, you could get to your destination faster (reward) but you also incur some risks: You could get in an accident and never make it to your destination; or you could get stopped by the police for speeding, pay a fine, get points added to your record, and be much later to arrive than had you stayed at the speed limit.

You may decide to compromise and drive a little over the speed limit, figuring that the police will not stop you, and you'll still get there a little sooner. This would be an optimal balance between risk and reward – take a conservative risk and achieve a comparable reward. Learning how to balance risk with reward is an efficient strategy in the world of investments.

Modern Portfolio Theory

When we as financial planners work to come up with an investment strategy, we run into the same problem as weather forecasters. We are trying to forecast the future but all we can do is look at the past. The meteorologists deal with this problem by carefully measuring previous behavior of weather indicators (wind speed and direction, air pressure, temperature, humidity, and so on), plugging the data into sophisticated computer models, and then generating probabilities for future events. For example, it might project a 60 percent chance of rain tomorrow. In the past, however, forecasters relied on unscientific (and unreliable) indicators such as a farmer's almanac or whether a groundhog saw its shadow on a particular day.

Financial planning has evolved as well. In the old days, investors depended on someone's ability to pick stocks or time the markets. Today, with the advent of **Modern Portfolio Theory**, and the ability to employ sophisticated computer models, investment planning is also now a science. Just like the meteorologist, we can carefully measure the movement of certain financial indicators, plug them into sophisticated computer models, and project the future behavior of these indicators with a defined degree of confidence.

In weather forecasting, certain underlying principles of physics make the forecasts possible. It is assumed to be normal, for example, that air moves from high pressure to low pressure, and that hot air rises. In investment planning there are also certain critical assumptions when employing Modern Portfolio Theory to make financial forecasts. These include the relationship between risk and return and the assumption that the portfolio to be measured is well diversified.

What Is Risk?

Risk is the chance of something causing harm or going wrong. In financial planning, it can also be defined as the chance that worrying about your investments will keep you up at night. Both of these definitions, however, are hard to measure with numbers and plug into a computer. So modern portfolio theory measures volatility of returns (standard deviation) and calls it "risk." The more an investment bounces up and down, the more uncertain its future value, the riskier it is.

Investment portfolios have two kinds of risks: systematic and unsystematic. **Systematic risk** is common to all securities in a given market and is similar to a tide. Regardless of how many or what kind of boats (investments) you have, they all go up and down with the tide. There is no way to avoid this risk other than to get out of the market (or the water). **Unsystematic risks** are associated with individual assets. What if the company you are investing in goes bankrupt and your stock becomes worthless? Unsystematic risk can be diversified away by including a number of different, non-correlated holdings in a portfolio. **Non-correlated** means the movement of one does not relate to the movement of the other; that is, they do not move up and down together. The more they differ in their movement, the less correlated they are. Think of a bunch of different boats (or investments) in choppy water. At any one time, some are moving up, others are moving down, bigger boats are moving less than smaller boats, etc. In a developed market, such as in the United States, holding 30-40 non-correlated securities will be sufficient to minimize unsystematic risk.

Because unsystematic risk is avoidable by diversifying your holdings, Modern Portfolio Theory does not deal with that risk. It quite reasonably assumes that you will make that risk go away by diversifying your portfolio. This assumption leads to two observations:

First – there is no "reward" or greater return expectation for taking on the risk of a concentrated (non-diversified) portfolio.

Second – we would be unable to make useful projections of that portfolio because Modern Portfolio Theory, upon which all forecasting models are based, assumes a well-diversified portfolio. It would be comparable to insisting that a meteorologist mix in Groundhog Day data with their weather forecasting models; it doesn't compute.

What Is Return?

A **reward** is a payoff – big or otherwise – for your efforts. Rewards can vary from hitting the million dollar jackpot by purchasing a $5 lottery ticket, to winning a scholarship because you are a star athlete, to getting a large commission for a sale, to purchasing a bond and having it pay off more than anticipated due to the decline in interest rates. Rewards can come through either hard work, taking calculated risks, sheer luck or a combination of these.

In financial terms, return or reward is defined as what you would expect to get from the portfolio in the future. Related to both risk and return is the price you would expect to pay for a security, or a portfolio of securities. The **Capital Asset Pricing Model**, which is based on Modern Portfolio Theory, states what we already know intuitively, that one can expect a higher return for riskier assets, but, as described above, only for those that have higher systematic risk.

Risk and Reward "Monopoly"

The concepts of the Capital Asset Pricing Model can be applied to a simple real estate transaction as well. Say you are considering purchasing two commercial real estate investments. Both generate $1 million in rents per year (after expenses of maintenance, taxes, and so forth). Building One is fully leased by a Fortune 500 drugstore for the next 15 years. Building Two is a half-vacant strip mall with stores such as nail boutiques, clothing shops, and small restaurants. The Building Two tenants all have short-term leases and none has a credit rating anywhere close to that of the large, publicly-traded company. Because the drug chain is a stable, good credit tenant, the risk is relatively low. That means you are willing to accept a 5 percent return on Building One, so you would pay $20 million for that building. However, because the risk on the half-empty strip mall is far greater, you would insist on a 20 percent return and would therefore only pay $500,000 for that building.

The Efficient Frontier and Risk-Free Return

Another concept is **risk-free return** (think U.S. Treasury bills) where your return is presumed to be without risk. If you are taking on risk, you should expect a return greater than the risk-free return. Otherwise, your investment would be "inefficient." On the other hand, if your portfolio has the lowest risk for a given return, or the highest return for a given risk, it would be "efficient." Plotting all the portfolios with the lowest risk and all the portfolios with the highest returns and finding their intersections is what's known as the **Efficient Frontier**.

Figure 7.1 illustrates how the Efficient Frontier enables investors to understand how a portfolio's expected returns vary with the amount of risk taken.

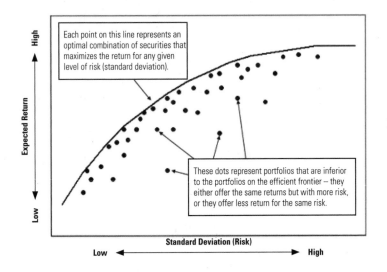

Figure 7.1. The Efficient Frontier
(Source: www.investinganswers.com)

Smart investors choose portfolios that generate the largest possible returns with the least amount of risk. In other words, they tend to seek portfolios on the Efficient Frontier. The ultimate goal in constructing a portfolio is to get it as close as possible to the Efficient Frontier, meaning your money is working as hard as it can for you.

Risks to Avoid

You might take an extraordinary risk if necessary – such as donating blood marrow or a kidney – to save the life of someone you love. The reward (seeing your loved one return to health) is important enough to justify the risk. However, taking a risk without the expectation of a comparable reward is foolhardy. Why would you ride your bicycle to school or work on a cold and rainy day when you could just as easily drive or take a bus?

Fundamental to the concept of "risk" is that you do not know the outcome. If you did, it would not be a risk, it would be a certainty. And risks have no guarantees. Investments in U.S. Treasury bonds are considered risk-free, if held to maturity because we are certain that the U.S. will pay its obligations. Just about any other investment has some uncertainty and therefore some risk.

Watch out for "get rich quick" schemes in which someone promises you huge returns on your investment. The only person getting rich is the one selling you the scheme. As the saying goes, if it sounds too good to be true, it probably is.

Try to make choices that keep you from being in a position where you have to get large returns and therefore take big risks. In the car speeding story at the beginning of this Lesson, the driver could have decided to leave earlier so that she would not be so late in the first place.

Risk Tolerance: Risks Worth Taking

Even when the risk is smaller, there are no guarantees. Except for U.S. Treasury bonds and federally-insured bank products, just about any investment has some uncertainty and therefore some risk.

Take risks that are reasonable in light of the return you are seeking. For example, a stock market risk is reasonable if you expect to get an 8 percent average return but is not justified if the best return you could expect would be 3 percent. There are other less risky choices that should give you a better return.

How much risk should you take with your investments?

If you are asking this question, then you are looking at the problem backwards. Start first with your goal. How much money do you need and when do you need it? Say you need $2 million in 30 years for retirement and you can save $800 per month and will increase the amount you are saving by 5 percent each year. Once you know this, your financial advisor can construct a portfolio that will get you to your goal with the highest degree of predictability (least amount of risk). In this example, you will need a portfolio that generates an average of 8 percent on its earnings per year. This means investing mostly in the stock market – a relatively high risk.

So, in essence, your goal determines your risk. If you cannot tolerate the risk necessary to get to your goal, then you need to adjust your goal or rethink your risk tolerance. If investing mostly in the stock market keeps you up at night then you need to rethink either your goal or the amount you are willing to save.

Risk and age

Generally, your willingness to accept large swings in your portfolio declines as you age. Once you are retired, for example, you are counting on your investments to pay your living expenses for the rest of your life and you have no way to replace large losses.

Those who take on the greatest risk often have a longer investment horizon, so they can afford to wait through market swings. Of course, there are 90-year-olds who still work or are financially independent and love putting any extra money into the stock market figuring that their children will reap the benefits. Once again, there is no hard and fast rule. If you have some extra money, and figure it's worth the gamble, then you can take the risk.

TIP FOR THE PARENT: The son observed: When I was in high school in the late '90's, I remember clearly that my "ABC" stock was going up precipitously, splitting eight ways in a year. There was the possibility that the "ABC" technology would be used for the cell phones in China, so people were buying the stock on the gamble that the deal might come through and the company would greatly expand. I remember that my grandfather, who'd lived through the Great Depression, always stuck to his stocks and never sold, even when he knew that they'd go down sometimes. As a result, granddad stuck to the stock long after his investment advisor had strongly recommended that he sell it, and it kept going up. The stock eventually plunged from its peak value, and lost much of its bubble worth. In this experience, I saw the value of sticking to a good stock over the long term and to avoid "playing the market," but at the same time, you have to be steeled against the violent ups and downs from momentarily popular stocks.

Take This to the Bank

- There is no reward without a risk.

- Balance risk and reward to manage uncertainty.

- If you take on a risk, make sure the reward is worth it.

- Your goals determine the amount of risk you must undertake.

- Truly know yourself in terms of your risk tolerance. Can you really sit still while the account goes down by 50 percent? A rule of thumb: Avoid the stock market unless you are willing to wait a long time to recover losses.

- Generally the smarter and better informed you are, the lower the risks.

- Choose carefully—just because you take a risk it does not guarantee a reward.

- Buy the steak, not the sizzle. Focus on substance and do not be swayed by fear, greed, or persuasion by the salesperson.

Parting Shot

Life is risk. The key to success is to make sure any risk you take on is for a comparable reward. The risk you need to tolerate is dictated by your goals. If you cannot tolerate the risk, moderate your goals. Design your portfolio to get you to your goals with the minimum risk necessary and then stay focused on your goals.

LESSONS TO MY CHILDREN

Learn Investing 101

And it won't make one bit of difference if I answer right
or wrong; when you're rich they think you really know.
"If I Were a Rich Man"

Fiddler on the Roof

Although the concept of investing may seem intimidating at first, it is actually fairly clear-cut and consists of three steps. First, come up with your goal and time frame: How much will you need and by when? Second, build a portfolio of investments designed to reach your objectives. Third and finally, monitor and adjust your portfolio every three months (quarterly).

The only reliable way to invest and build wealth towards a goal is to invest in a diverse group of **non-correlated** investments – your portfolio. Non-correlated simply means that the investments do not move up and down at the same time. Taken as a whole, the returns of the group should be much more predictable than the individual investments.

The process of building a portfolio involves selecting the categories of investments you think will work best and then testing the portfolio using computer statistical modeling programs. This process is usually done by a financial planner, and going into the details of the statistical modeling is beyond the scope of this book. However, you'll need to understand the most common investments found in a portfolio. In particular, how and where cash, stocks, bonds, mutual funds, index funds, and real estate fit into the overall picture.

Get Your Priorities in Order

First priority: Invest in yoursel; build the engine for future returns

What follows is a classic (and some say legendary) example of what **not** to do: While touring China, a businessman came upon a team of nearly 100 workers building an earthen dam with shovels. The businessman commented to a local official that, with an earth-moving machine, a single worker could create the dam in an afternoon. The official's curious response was, "Yes, but think of all the unemployment that would cause." "Oh," said the businessman, "I thought you were building a dam. If you want to create jobs, then take away their shovels and give them spoons!"

The same applies to your own life. If you want to build a dam, you need to invest in earth-moving machinery. If you want to create wealth, you need to invest in your primary engine of wealth creation – yourself. Once you find your passion and know the field you want to work in, get the highest level of education and certification that you can. Put yourself in a position to be highly sought-after and respected. As long as you are going to be working for a living, you might as well do something you love, get paid well, and fulfill your potential. If your passion is small animals, for example, become an outstanding veterinarian, and make it your life's work.

Investing in yourself continues throughout your entire life. The authors have the highest degrees and credentials in their fields, but still spend about one hour per day learning and trying to keep up with current developments.

Second priority: Get a steady job

Unless you just inherited wealth or won the lottery, you cannot start an investment/wealth creation plan until you have a steady job that pays enough to cover your expenses and your savings plan. There are many books and Web sites that can provide assistance with this.

Third priority: Save six months' worth of living expenses

Unexpected expenses will come up from time to time. It's impossible to manage a goal-oriented savings plan if you have to keep spending your investment funds on emergencies. So before beginning an investment plan, first put aside enough savings to cover six months' worth of living expenses. Make it a priority to replenish the "emergency fund" whenever it falls below the target.

Fourth priority: Start your investment program

So you have completed your formal education and the certifications needed to set you on your desired career path. You have a well-paying, steady job, and have been able to save six months' worth of living expenses in your emergency fund. Now it is time to start investing.

Design a Portfolio to Meet Your Goal(s)

When designing a portfolio, three time frames come into play:

- Short-Term: up to two years

- Medium-Term: two to ten years

- Long-Term: more than ten years.

These time frames are the single most important element in designing a portfolio that will achieve investing goals. Keep in mind that a "long-term" goal will convert to a "medium-term" goal when the goal is five years away, and again to a "short-term" when the goal is two years away. Let's say you have a baby and when the youngster turns three, your goal is college for the child in 15 years when she is age 18. Your time frame is "long-term" until the child turns 13. At that point, your time frame is "medium-term" and the portfolio needs to be adjusted accordingly. When the child turns 16, the time frame is "short-term" and the portfolio needs to be adjusted once again.

Use the following to help you assess the fit of investments for your portfolio. Different types of investments will be discussed further in this Lesson.

Short-term goals, under two years. These should be cash-like investments. They are liquid, well protected against losses, but also give you relatively poor returns and lose value when there is inflation. A short-term goal is less of an investment and more like an extension of your savings plan.

Medium-term goals, two to ten years. Consider the bigger economic environment, and adjust the investments to the market cycle, paying close attention to whether it's going up or down. Does everything seem to be going up? If you invest in such a market, watch it closely and be prepared to pull everything out at the first sign of a downslide as there will be insufficient time to recover from large losses. A financial advisor or other investment expert can help you make decisions based on shifts in the stock market, which are complex and depend upon many factors. You need to get close to your goal amount two years before your target date because you will be shifting to more conservative investments when your time frame becomes "short-term."

Long-term goals, over ten years. With these goals, market cycles are not a concern and can be ridden out. Focus on investments appropriate for reaching your goal based in the individual characteristics of the investment.

Overall Characteristics of Investments

Before discussing the particulars of stocks, bonds, mutual funds, and other types of investments, you'll need to understand how each fits into a diverse portfolio. **Diversification** is critical to your choices and involves investing in a variety of financial instruments, including stocks, bonds, commodities and even real estate.

Characteristics of investments include:

- *Liquidity.* **Liquid investments** are easy to buy, sell, and convert to cash without penalties or losses.

Examples include publicly-traded stocks and mutual funds. The most liquid assets are currency, money held in bank accounts, checks and money orders. **Illiquid investments** are difficult to buy and sell and include things like Certificates of Deposit (CDs) and real estate. Cashing in a CD early will cause a penalty of up to six months of interest. Selling a house often takes months to get a fair price.

- *Volatility.* How much does the investment move up and down? Stocks move a lot, cash does not move at all.

- *Income.* Does the investment pay any income? How much of the expected return is in the form of regular cash flow? How is the income taxed?

- *Growth.* Is the investment expected to grow in value? Is growth a major component of the investment's return?

- *Correlation.* How does it fit in the portfolio? Does it enhance diversification? For financial analysis purposes, correlation is measured on a scale from 1 to -1. A "1" means the two are exactly correlated. A "0" means that there is no correlation at all – considered desirable in a portfolio – and a "-1" means inverse correlation; that is, when one changes, the other goes in the opposite direction.

- *Inflation.* Does the asset protect you against loss of value during inflation?

- *Certainty.* Do you get back the amount you started with, regardless of whether it still has the same purchasing power? Cash held in a federally insured bank account has "certainty," but may not be "safe" in the context of getting you to your financial goal.

- *Business Risk.* How does it fare when the underlying company becomes insolvent or bankrupt?

Using the concepts above, Figure 8.1 illustrates the differences in each kind of investment.

	Cash	Stocks	Bonds	Mutual and Index Funds	Real Estate (REITs)	Annuities
Liquidity	High	High	Med	High	Low	Low
Volatility	None	High	Med	Depends	Med	Low
Income	Low	Low	High	Depends	Med	N/A
Growth	None	Med	Low	Depends	Med	N/A
Correlation	N/A	N/A	Low	Depends	Low	N/A
Inflation	Poor	Good	Poor	Depends	Good	Depends
Certainty	High	None	High	Depends	Poor	Good
Business Risk	Low	High	Med	None	Low	Low

Figure 8.1. Investments and Their Characteristics

Cash

Cash means savings deposits, certificates of deposit (CDs), and money market mutual funds.

Bottom line: Cash is secure, liquid, and certain. Use it for when you are getting close to needing to spend for short-term goals. Otherwise, it has no use in a long- or medium-term investment portfolio.

Stocks

Publicly-traded stocks, the kind you can buy and sell through a brokerage firm or an on-line trading account, are typically the foundation of a long-term investment portfolio. They can be sliced and diced a number of ways, depending on your objective. You can divide stocks by "sector" meaning type of industry (such as, utilities, transportation, industrial, technology, and so on); by geography (domestic, foreign, international, emerging markets, Pacific Rim, and so on); by size (large cap, small cap, medium cap, and so on); or by style (growth, value, or a blend of the two).

Cap is short for "Market Capitalization" which means the value of all the shares currently held by investors. A "large cap" company is found on major stock indices like the Standard & Poor (S&P) 500 index, or the Dow. The Dow Jones Industrial Average is the 30 largest companies in the United States and they have an average market capitalization of $120 billion. The S&P 500 is comprised of the 500 leading U.S. companies with a market cap of $3.5 billion or more. Small cap firms have under $1 billion in shares held by investors and are typically found in the Russell 2000 index or the S&P Small Cap 600. Medium cap firms (between small and large) are typically found in the Russell Midcap and the S&P 400 Midcap index.

Stocks are considered to be an inflation hedge. They do well in an inflationary environment and are expected to produce returns, mostly growth, that will outpace inflation. Historically, a well-diversified stock portfolio produces between 7 – 10 percent average annual growth. Inflation has averaged 3 percent. Of course, historical numbers hardly guarantee future performance, and because stocks are so volatile, they are unsuitable for short- or medium-term time frames. If the company you own stock in goes bankrupt, your stock becomes worthless. That is why you want to make sure that no single stock (or any other single investment, for that matter) makes up more than 2 percent of your portfolio.

Bottom line: Stocks are the foundation for a long-term growth-oriented portfolio.

TIP FOR THE PARENT: The daughter remembered in 7th grade how she had to pick a stock of a particular company and track the progress (or lack thereof) for a school project. After talking about this project with her parents, her mom suggested she pick a stock for the school project that she actually already owned, Pepsi. She still remembered that during the time that she was tracking the stock and doing the project, the stock split and she was super excited. She learned a lot about stocks in that project. If your child's school does not do such a project, you can do a similar thing with your child at home and make it a contest or game.

Bonds

When you buy a bond, you are loaning your money to a company or government entity. You expect to get interest on your loan, also known as **yield**. At the maturity of the bond you should get back the face amount of the bond plus the yield.

Most bonds are issued in denominations of $10,000 and mature in 30 years. Bond prices, however, are quoted on a $100 scale. For example, say you buy a bond priced at $76 (a 24 percent discount). Assuming the company remains able to meet debts (solvent), you will redeem the bond at its face value ($100) upon maturity, and make a nice capital gain in addition to the interest payments. Likewise, if you were to buy a bond at $105, you are paying a 5 percent premium above face value. At maturity you will still only get back the $100. Obviously, you would only buy a bond at a premium if you thought the bond's interest payment more than makes up for the capital loss at maturity.

Bond prices fluctuate based upon changes in the credit of the company issuing the bond, the time until maturity, and the interest rate. As interest rates go up, bond prices go down and vice versa. The longer the time until maturity, the bigger the swings in value. If you hold the bond until maturity and then cash it in for its face value, fluctuations in price won't matter, but most investors plan to cash them sooner and must consider fund volatility.

Bonds are rated by a credit rating agency, such as Moody's, on the credit quality of the issuing company. An "investment grade" bond has a high credit rating and means the company or government entity issuing the bond can offer a lower interest rate or yield. Lower credit companies have to offer higher interest rates to sell their bonds. These are known as **high yield** or **junk**

bonds. Bonds issued by the Federal government (Treasuries) and by federal agencies (such as Sally Mae or Freddy Mac) have the highest credit because nobody expects the government to default on its obligations. Therefore, they tend to have lower yields.

State and municipal bonds **(muni-bonds)** have a unique feature – their interest is free of federal income tax. If you pay income taxes to the state that issued the bond, the bonds are free of state tax as well. For example, if you live in Virginia and buy a Richmond, Virginia muni-bond, you pay no income tax on the interest. Because of their tax preferred status, they offer a lower yield. To compare a muni-bond to any other taxable bond, you need to adjust for the taxes you would pay on the other bond's interest. If, however, you buy a muni-bond at a discount and later sell if for a gain, the capital gains are not tax free at either the federal or state level, only the interest.

Bottom Line: Bonds add diversity to a long- and medium-term portfolio, but may not perform well in a financial environment with inflation or rising interest rates.

Mutual Funds, Both Actively Managed and Passive (Index)

A **mutual fund** is a company that pools investor money to buy a portfolio of securities. There are over 14,000 mutual funds. Most funds have a particular emphasis like "large cap stocks" or "international stocks" or "junk bonds" or "technology stocks" and so on. A large cap stock fund, for example, will buy predominantly large cap stocks. These funds usually choose an index to serve as their **benchmark**, a standard by which to judge how well the fund is doing, which allows investors to compare their performance. For example, a U.S. large cap stock fund might choose the S&P 500 index as its benchmark.

An **index fund** is a passive type of mutual fund whose investment objective is to achieve approximately the same return as a particular market index, such as the S&P 500, the Russell 2000 Index, or others. An index fund will attempt to achieve its investment objective primarily by investing in the securities (stocks or bonds) of companies that are included in a selected index. Some index funds invest in all of the companies included in an index; others only invest in a portion.

An actively managed mutual fund is managed by a fund manager who is paid to pick selected securities for the fund. In contrast, an index fund is not actively managed. It simply purchases the stocks in the index. Because the index fund does not pay for active management, its expenses are significantly lower. The only reason you would go with the more expensive, actively-managed mutual fund is to receive greater value than the index in terms of total returns, lower risk or some combination of the two. Among actively managed funds, achieving better than benchmark results, however, is elusive. Most actively-managed funds underperform their benchmark over long periods of time.

When you invest in a mutual fund or index fund, you are buying shares in the company that sponsors the fund. Your shares are re-priced daily to reflect the underlying value of the holdings of the fund. For example, say you buy $1,000 of a Russell 2000 Index fund and the stocks in the index go up 5 percent that day. At the end of the day your shares would be priced at $1,050, up 5 percent.

There are many ways to evaluate a mutual fund. You can find the fund's performance track record, peer ranking and expense ratio relative to other funds with similar objectives, risk-adjusted performance, and adherence to its style or objective to name just a few. Unfortunately, past performance measures do not always have positive predictive value. About the best that can be said is that bad performance numbers or excessive expenses are predictors for continued bad performance. Use past performance only as a negative screen to rule out poor performing funds.

Once you have dropped the funds with poor performance numbers, you are left with the (historically) good performers. But this is as far as you can go with quantitative measures. A history of good performance is not a reliable predictor of continued good performance. The key to finding a good mutual fund is to realize that when you buy a mutual fund you are buying a manager, not just the underlying securities that the company is managing. Evaluate the manager like you would any other manager looking at qualitative measures such as: How well run is the company? Do they have good governance? Is there a low turnover of key personnel? Is there a good corporate culture? Are their investment processes well-defined, clearly articulated, and followed? Do they have good risk controls in place? Do they have a good growth path for their best employees or do those employees have to leave to get promoted? How much of the manager's personal net worth is invested in the success of the fund he is managing? How is the compensation of the manager and analysts tied to the performance of the fund portfolio? What is the company's regulatory track record?

If you want to beat the benchmark you will need to do your homework or work with a financial advisor who can look beyond quantitative numbers and research how the mutual fund company is managed. Otherwise, accept market performance and stick with index funds.

Bottom Line: Mutual funds and index funds are a great way to start investing. They allow you to obtain professional management and diversification with small amounts of money.

Real Estate Investments

For most families, their house is their single biggest and most important investment. While your house is a place where you live, you should nevertheless keep an eye towards resale whenever you are thinking of home improvements. That bright yellow and purple paint scheme you saw on a home decorating channel might look great on a TV show, but few will purchase a house with such décor. Keeping your house neat, attractive, and uncluttered not only makes it a more pleasant place to live, it enhances its value.

You can also invest in real estate over and above your house or condominium. Investment real estate falls into two broad categories: residential rentals and commercial properties. **Residential rentals** are popular among individual investors, but are difficult to manage and must greatly increase in value in order to get a decent return on their investment. Buying and managing **commercial real estate** is even more complicated and can be a full-time career in and of itself.

The best way to get an allocation of real estate in your portfolio is through a REIT. A **REIT (Real Estate Investment Trust)** is a company that pools investor money to buy and sell commercial real estate properties, a kind of mutual fund for real estate. In fact, the main reason a REIT is used for real estate, rather than a mutual fund, is that a REIT can pass the losses associated with real estate (such as depreciation and property taxes) out to the investors. This helps investors reduce their taxes. A mutual fund cannot pass losses on to investors.

Two types of REITs are available to most investors: Publicly-traded and public non-traded REITs. **Publicly-traded REITs** are just like any stock in the stock market. Most of the benefit of being in real estate is lost because these REITs behave like stocks.

The correlation between the Dow Jones U.S. Select REIT index and the S&P 500 index for the last 5 years is 0.8. This means that the movement of the S&P 500 dictates the movement of the publicly-traded REITs 80 percent of the time. Because publicly-traded REITs are so close to stocks in their behavior, we think of them as stocks in terms of how they fit in a portfolio.

Public Non-traded REITs are just that, they are not traded on an exchange. They are sold through the broker/dealer or investment advisor channels. Like the publicly-traded REITs and mutual funds, they pool investor money to buy and sell commercial real estate, but the value of your holdings will be more directly tied to the value of the underlying real estate. It is subject to fluctuations in real estate values, but not the stock market. This makes it a real estate investment more than a stock or mutual fund and gives your portfolio its desired diversification. The correlation between commercial real estate holdings (NCREIF index) and U.S. stocks (S&P 500) for the last five years was -0.11, and fixed income bonds (BarCap U.S. Agg Bond index) was -0.13 which essentially means there was little correlation between real estate and either stocks or bonds.

Bottom Line: Real estate is a great non-correlated addition to a long-term investment portfolio.

Annuities

An **annuity** is a contract with an insurance company in which you agree to make one or more payments to them, and in turn they agree to pay you one or more payments in the future, most typically an income stream for a stated period of time. If the payments start right away, then it is an **immediate annuity**. If the payments start at some point in the future, it is a **deferred**

annuity. **Fixed annuities** pay you a fixed rate of interest that may reset periodically and the principal does not fluctuate. In contrast, **variable annuities** have no fixed rate of interest and your principal rises or falls with the markets. Both fixed and variable annuities allow you to accumulate tax-deferred funds for a certain number of years, then give you the option of withdrawing the accumulated amount or converting it into an income stream for life (annuitizing). Some variable annuities provide certain guaranteed withdrawal amounts or income benefits, like fixed annuities.

Annuities have their drawbacks, however. They may be 2 to 3 percent more expensive per year than a comparable mutual fund. Also, they have significant restrictions on liquidity. Your ability to get your money back in a lump sum is limited and if you need to take your money early, you could pay penalties as high as 10 percent. Once the annuity is paying you the income stream for life, you have no ability to accelerate those payments and just get all the cash. Yet, having a guaranteed income stream is important enough to some investors who prefer to avoid risk.

Bottom Line: Annuities can be part of an investment portfolio. They are more expensive and less liquid than mutual funds, but they can provide you with an income for life or term certain, provided the insurance company remains solvent.

Accredited-Only Investments

The Securities and Exchange Commission (SEC) divides investors into two categories: accredited and non-accredited. An **accredited investor** is simply a person (or married couple) with: a net worth of $1 million or more; or income of over

$200,000 for the last two years or joint income with that person's spouse in excess of $300,000 in each of those years and a reasonable expectation of reaching the same income level in the current year. If you do not meet these criteria, you are a **non-accredited** investor. The reason behind this distinction is that an accredited investor is assumed to have the knowledge and/or resources to evaluate more complex investments and make sure that they are suitable. The following are examples of investment categories typically only available to accredited investors:

1. Managed Futures Funds

2. Direct Placement Programs

    a. Certain real estate investments

    b. Certain equipment leasing

    c. Certain oil and gas partnerships

3. Hedge Funds

4. Private Equity Funds

It is beyond the scope of this book to delve into these accredited-only investments. However, once you attain the status of an accredited investor, seek out a knowledgeable investment advisor with access to these types of investments. When employed properly, accredited-only investments can enhance the stability and performance of a portfolio.

Leverage and Investments

Mike's Story

In the late '90s, Mike struck investment gold. He was buying tech stocks on margin – essentially borrowing money to make money – and quickly amassed a fortune. His account held $5 million in tech stocks and $2.5 million in margin debt. He could have liquidated everything in the account and retired with $2.5 million. Instead, the tech bubble burst and his holdings quickly dropped to $2 million. But he could not keep the $2 million. He had to sell all of his stock to pay back the margin loan and continued to owe an additional $500,000, a debt that he is still paying off to this day.

Personal debt was discussed in Lesson 5. However, investment debt is different. When you borrow money to buy an investment, you accelerate your gains and losses, making the returns much more volatile. For example, say you purchase a commercial building for $1 million. You can either pay all cash or borrow $800,000 and pay in only $200,000 of your own money. Using debt, you can buy four more buildings the same way with your remaining $800,000.

But what happens when the building goes up or down in value? If the building goes up 20 percent and you sell it for $1.2 million, then you have made a 20 percent return in the all-cash case, but in the leveraged case you have doubled your money – a 100 percent return! (Actually, you need to pay interest on the debt so the return is a little less than 100 percent, but still really good.)

If the building goes down 20 percent and you sell it for $800,000 then you have lost 20 percent in the all-cash case. But in the leveraged case you have lost all your equity! The $800,000 proceeds from the sale will go to pay back the debt. If the building drops below 80 percent of its value, not only will you lose your investment, but if the debt is a recourse debt (discussed in Lesson 5), you may still owe the lender the balance due on the loan.

The same holds true for margin in a stock trading account. A **margin account** allows you to borrow up to half of the value of the investments in your account to buy more securities. But if they go down in value, you will get the dreaded **margin call** forcing you to sell the investments and perhaps also pay down the margin loan from your other assets. There is no such thing as a "non-recourse" margin account.

Some types of investments are only traded in margin accounts. Examples include options or commodities. Others, like commercial real estate, are typically traded using leverage, hopefully with controls in place to manage the added risk. Generally, unless you are a sophisticated investor with adequate controls for the inherent risks of leverage, avoid using debt to buy your investments. The chance for big profits is not worth the risk of total loss. Only use leverage for investments where you are willing to accept a total loss.

Watch Out for Ponzi Schemes!

A **Ponzi scheme** is an investment fraud that involves the payment of purported returns to existing investors from funds contributed by new investors. Ponzi scheme organizers often solicit new investors by promising to invest funds in opportunities claimed to generate high returns with little or no risk. In many Ponzi schemes, the fraudsters focus on attracting new money to make promised payments to earlier-stage investors. They often use funds for personal expenses, rather than engaging in any legitimate investment activity.

For example, say someone approaches you with an investment that involves paying 20 percent annual returns with no risk. You are excited to participate, forgetting the adage that if it sounds too good to be true, it probably is. But much to your amazement, you start getting statements showing a 20 percent return. You can even get the 20 percent paid to you if you ask for it. You start telling all your friends about the investment and they too want in. They tell all their friends and so on. But here's the thing – the Ponzi perpetrator is not investing the money. Rather, he or she is faking the statements and when an investor asks for the money, the fraudster either gives you back part of your initial investment and when that runs out, someone else's money. Eventually enough investors ask for money and the scheme collapses. There's nothing left and the fraudster goes to jail.

The easiest way to avoid a Ponzi scheme is to make sure that the company giving you the investment advice has your money held at a third-party custodian, which is not owned or controlled by the investment manager or financial advisor. The largest four third-party custodians are Fidelity, Pershing, Schwab and TD Ameritrade. As a client, you get statements from the third-party custodian as well as from the financial advisor. Any faked statements by the investment advisor would be immediately apparent.

The example of **Bernard Madoff** illustrates the ability of a Ponzi scheme to delude both individual and institutional investors as well as securities authorities for long periods. Madoff's version of the Ponzi was the **largest financial investor fraud** in history committed by a single person. Prosecutors estimate losses totaling $64.8 billion.

TIP FOR THE PARENT: The son wrote: When we owned stocks, Dad did his best to explain them to us and to make sure that we knew what stocks we had and how they were doing. We had to read the quarterly reports from each of the companies whose stocks we owned. I liked the fact that I had "XYZ" Company stock that made food and drinks, because the report came in a very glossy brochure and showed me all the food and drink brands that I partially owned. I liked the idea that if I ate some of the food or drink, the profits would eventually come back to me, even if in infinitesimally small portions – maybe a cent in my lifetime? It was cool that I could be paying myself back for eating.

Take This to the Bank

- Before investing in a portfolio, make sure your finances, personal life, and career are in order.

- Consider the amount of time you'll need to reach your financial goals when choosing investments.

- Certain types of investments have certain characteristics – compare and contrast the various features. Which best suits your needs?

- Regarding mutual funds, while bad performance numbers are usually a forecast of more of the same, good performance numbers are unreliable predictors of continued good performance.

- Investors wanting to avoid risks may prefer higher-priced annuities.

- Stocks are for long-term growth towards a goal.

- Cash is for immediate needs and short-term goals.

- Bonds and real estate add welcome diversification to a long-term portfolio.

- Long-term investors will ride out fluctuations in the stock market.

- Leverage accelerates both the good and the bad.

- The time frame for your goal is the most important element controlling the design of your portfolio.

Parting Shot

There is a lot more to investing than buying a few funds and hoping for the best. A financial advisor or other expert in the field can also be immensely helpful with this (see Lesson 9).

There are many good reasons to build an investment portfolio – for additional education, that dream house, to open your own business, and eventually for retirement. Perhaps most importantly, an investment portfolio can help you live debt free.

However, before you start investing, make sure you fulfill the four priorities outlined in this Lesson. Also follow the old adage "Don't put all your eggs in one basket," by diversifying your investments with an eye to short-, medium-, and long-term goals.

Assemble Your Team of Experts

Employ your time in improving yourself by other men's writings so you shall come easily by what others have labored hard for.

Socrates

Due to the rapid spread of technology, there has been a tremendous explosion of information and knowledge. This makes life more complex, which is where advisors come in. These experts will sit down and help you figure out what is best for you, based on your needs and desires. However, you'll need to know what to look for to locate those who can help you rather than just take your money.

While Americans tend to idealize the totally self-reliant, rugged individual, the truth is that success is a group effort. You did not get where you are today without the help of others and you will not get where you want to be without their assistance as well. (And in turn, you'll hopefully help others also.) Understanding what you do not know and the areas where you require help is the foundation of wisdom. Seek advice and guidance from experts and you will be well on your way to ensuring both personal and financial success.

John's Story

I was on vacation and dined often with a couple that had done well in the corporate world. He had a CPA doing his taxes, a lawyer doing his estate planning and two brokers competing against each other for his accounts. I asked him how much he paid for services. He said he knew what the legal services cost because there was a bill and it was the same for the tax work. I asked about his investment advisors and I was amazed to learn he had no idea what he was paying. He had never asked.

Your Circle of Advisors

What follows is a diagram of professionals that you may turn to at various points in time. You may deal with some, such as a financial planner or tax advisor, regularly and develop a long-term relationship. Others, such as a realtor, may be a one-shot deal.

- Financial planner
- Attorney

- Tax advisor (not just a preparer)
- Insurance agent
- Banker
- Real estate advisor/agent

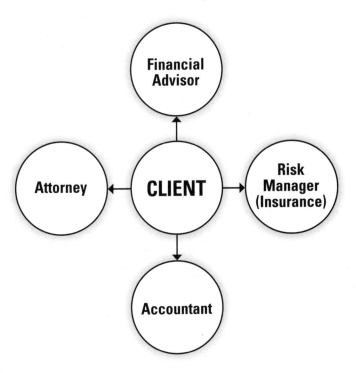

Figure 9.1. Circle of Advisors

Before You Begin...

Look for someone you can trust.

The first criterion when choosing advisors is **trust**, because you need to be sure they have your best interests in mind.

Rather than going for what seems to be the cheapest, look for the best, the one who puts your interest first, but does not offer or claim to be doing it all for free, since "free" usually just means the cost is hidden.

Find someone who will listen to you.

Make sure they are someone who will help you find solutions to your problems. How do you feel working with this expert? If the answer is "uncomfortable," then look for another one. Also, just as if you were consulting a physician for a health issue, you might also shop around and ask for a second opinion.

Prepare your questions ahead of time.

During the interview – and you almost always should meet your potential advisors face-to-face – have your questions prepared ahead of time. Look not only at what they say in response to your questions but at their facial expressions and body language and how they approach the questions and relate to you.

Check out the credentials of any advisor.

Do they have the highest degrees or certifications in their field? This includes examining the degrees on the wall, doing a Web search to make sure they are a Certified Public Accountant (CPA), or if a lawyer or insurance agent, have been admitted to the bar or licensed to sell insurance in your state. Although none of these qualifications is a guarantee that the advisor will successfully meet your needs, they do provide a measure of safety and quality assurance. Doing your homework will also help uncover any record of problems with previous clients.

Consider their experience.

How long have they been working in their field? It generally takes 10,000 hours or five years of full-time employment for a person to truly become an expert. But on the other side of the spectrum, how resistant are they to new ways of thinking? Some experts who have been around for decades may rest on their laurels and get mentally lazy.

Talk to their references.

Why did they choose this expert? What was their experience? Was there anything about their experience that was special? Disappointing? Surprising? Would they do it again?

Is the advisor up-to-speed?

This is the Internet age. Do they provide you with online access to view your accounts and watch the activity? Does your financial advisor send out periodic reports on performance? Does your accountant or attorney tell you when the law changes in a way that is important to you?

Using and Selecting Advisors

Although it's good to try to take care of things on your own, if you feel you might be getting in over your head or are unsure about something, then it's time to start thinking about obtaining some outside guidance, even if you have to spend money to do so. It is far better to learn from another's mistakes than from your own. "Doing it yourself" can only take you so far, especially when dealing with complex personal and financial issues.

In selecting advisors, look for those who win when you win and hurt when you hurt. Their interests need to be aligned with yours.

Wes' Story

As a professional, I see this at least once a month. A prospective client walks in and asks what does it cost for a legal, tax, or financial work before I know anything more than their name, address and phone number. I have found that the only correct answer is to say you were told my hourly rate or that this was a courtesy consult, but I cannot tell you more than that until we have talked enough for me to understand what you need and what your objectives are. Once I know what you need, I can tell you whether we offer that service and how we would take care of your legal, tax or financial matter. You can then chose to engage us or not at that time. That is safe for you the client and also for the professional as he is not shooting from the hip, but rather getting to know you well enough to find the right solution for you and not just the standard boiler plate.

Financial planner. The financial planner's job is to provide you objective and personalized advice on how to best structure your investments so that you will reach your goals. The financial planner should also be able to implement the advice, make the buys and sells, provide ongoing performance monitoring, and periodically review the plan to see if you are still on track, or update the plan if your goals have changed.

When choosing a financial advisor, find out how he or she gets paid. If it's based on commission, what guarantee do you have that their advice is good for you and not just for their monthly commission report? And, also as discussed earlier, nothing in this world is for free – usually the fee is buried in the fine print or hidden in the purchase price.

Richard's Story

Historically, I was a buy and hold securities investor. One day I took a call from the broker's new sales assistant who suggested I buy a dotcom mutual fund. I elected to take his advice even though I had no real dealings with this assistant before. Only when I later became a broker did I realize that the broker owed me no duty of care other than that the product he sold to me had to be suitable at the time of sale. The broker had no duty to tell me when to get out, or to disclose any conflict of interest. When the dotcom bubble burst, he had won and I had lost.

Third-party custodians are valuable. Be wary of an advisor who actually holds your money or securities and reports on them as opposed to those who have them held by third-party custodians the largest four of which include Fidelity, Pershing, Schwab and TD Ameritrade. These third-party custodians, can verify separately what is going on. Those who entrusted their money to Madoff learned that lesson the hard way.

Make sure the advisor has the proper credentials. Along with receiving a Bachelor's degree or higher from an accredited college or university, advisors who are Certified Financial Planners® (CFPs), have met stringent requirements in the areas of education, examination, experience and ethics (known as "the four Es") from the Certified Financial Planner Board of Standards, the field's regulatory organization. You can ask for a membership card or check them out on the CFP Web site (www.cfp.net).

If your advisor is going to buy and sell securities for you through a broker/dealer channel, he or she should also have their Series 7 and 66 FINRA licenses. The largest independent regulator for securities firms in the United States, the Financial Industry Regulatory Authority (FINRA) is dedicated to investor protection and market integrity. You can also go to the FINRA Web site (www.finra.org) to see if the advisor has any record of complaints.

Financial Products are Delivered Through Four Channels.

A broker/dealer (B/D) channel.

A B/D channel is a financial-products sales channel. The broker is compensated by a combination of sales commissions, product trails, and product loads. A **trail** is a small ongoing fee paid to the broker who sold you the product. It is usually between ¼ and 1 percent. A **load** is an upfront fee paid to the broker who sold you the product. Loads typically range from 3 to 10 percent.

If the product is proprietary to a particular B/D channel, there may be other costs associated with it as well; expenses can be hidden in voluminous prospectuses and can be challenging to find. And the only legal duty the broker has to you is to ensure that the product they are selling to you is suitable **at the time**. After that point, they have no other responsibilities regarding your financial best interests.

As long as you understand you are responsible for making all decisions about what to buy and sell, you can take advantage of certain financial products that are only available through a B/D channel. If you want to invest directly in real estate, for example, you can buy into a real estate partnership sold as a security. You are entitled to rely on the facts stated in the prospectus, and upon the B/D's due diligence in looking at the investment. If you try to buy into such a partnership on your own and not as a security, you have only yourself to rely upon. Brokers can also be a resource for research and information about financial products.

The insurance channel.

Life insurance and annuities are often sold as financial products. This is another commission sales channel where the costs are almost entirely hidden. You would be hard-pressed to find out how much of your insurance premium actually goes into the company's insurance reserves and how much goes to the salesperson. When you buy an insurance product you are paying in part for the transfer of risk to the insurance company. That generally makes these products more expensive, but if insurance guarantees are valuable to you, they are worth the price. If you are just looking for investments, other channels will be better.

The banking channel.

Banks have always been in the business of lending money and paying interest on deposits, but they have recently gone into the securities business and tend to adopt the broker/dealer model, which involves a commission.

The registered investment advisor (RIA) channel.

Of the four channels, the RIA is the only one who is acknowledged to be a **fiduciary** to their clients. As a fiduciary, the RIA has a duty to put the client's interest first, to fully disclose all fees, and to avoid conflicts of interest. It is easy to compare cost and value in the RIA channel.

Attorney. Your attorney is responsible for advising you on how to structure your legal affairs so he or she best serves your interests. Your attorney will also implement your legal planning by drafting documents and representing you in transactions and disputes. Like doctors, attorneys that understand financial planning usually call themselves "trust and estate" attorneys. They handle estate and trust administration, tax planning, asset protection, and trust and estate controversies. They can draft trusts, wills, and powers of attorney; administer estates; represent you if there is a fight among the beneficiaries; and do taxes. Most trust and estate attorneys do not, for example, handle real estate closings or divorces. Your attorney is automatically a fiduciary; that is, he or she is acting in your best interest and is required to avoid (or fully disclose) any conflict of interest and preserve your confidences.

Lawyers should have at least a J.D. (Juris Doctor) degree from an accredited law school and be an active member of the state bar. A Masters of Law (LL.M.) is a plus, if it's relevant to your issue. You can check out lawyers at http://www.abanet.org/, or http://www.martindale.com/, or the state bar for your state.

Tax expert. If your taxes are simple – say you have a full-time job with steady withholding and a minimum of routine deductions – you might be able to do your own income tax return by using software programs such as TurboTax. But to be safe (and to avoid getting unnecessary attention from the IRS), have a tax professional review it to see if you missed anything and redo it if necessary. Once the return starts getting complicated, however, you will probably need the services of a tax professional, either a tax lawyer or Certified Public Accountant (CPA). Like lawyers, CPAs are fiduciaries bound by strict rules of professional responsibility. They have a duty to look out for your best interests and avoid any conflicts of interest. Many people think of tax preparation as an annual event. However, a good accountant or tax lawyer can help monitor your tax, legal, personal and financial circumstances throughout the year, giving you an opportunity to address ongoing tax issues rather than just report them. Regardless of who you choose, make sure your preparer signs the return, is licensed, is open year-round, and gets paid a set fee for services rather than a percentage of the refund.

It pays to obtain the services of a CPA or tax lawyer, especially if your taxes are the least bit complicated. In one study by the General Accounting Office, employees posed as taxpayers and visited several tax preparation chains in a large metropolitan area. The chains made errors on many of the returns, computing wrong refund and overpayment amounts, some of which were in excess of several thousand dollars. In another study, the Treasury Inspector General for Administration (TIGTA) had auditors pose as taxpayers. They visited 12 commercial chains and 16 small independently owned tax preparation offices also in a big city. Not only were the tax preparers unlicensed and not legally "enrolled" for practice before the IRS, but 61 percent of the returns were incorrectly prepared.

Insurance agent. Insurance is used for risk management. As you go through life, marry, have a family, and so on, you'll find that your risk management needs will change. However, the insurance industry is based upon commission sales, which means there is a built-in conflict of interest between you and the insurance salesperson. There are, however, good insurance professionals who will give you solid advice and when you locate such an individual, include them in your circle of advisors.

For an insurance agent, you want someone who cares about you and your family and will be responsive in case of a claim. The agent or agency must, of course, be licensed by the state for their type of insurance.

Others. At different points in your life you may have need for a banker, real estate advisor, or even a charitable organization development office, such as an alumni association if you decide to donate substantial funds to your alma mater. As with the other advisors, carefully consider their qualifications and whether they seem to have your best interests at heart. For example, when selecting a realtor to sell your home, find someone with has a reputation and statistics for the following:

- Short-average time from listing to sale

- Sales price close to listed price

- Several referrals by satisfied clients

- An inexpensive, fast, and reliable repair person who can help get the property ready for sale

---

Start Building Your Team!

It's never too early to start thinking about the future and how advisors can help you reach your goals. The following steps will help you get started in building your circle of advisors.

1. Make a list of your current complex financial, legal, insurance and tax issues.

2. Grade yourself on how many you think you have the time or expertise to answer.

3. For those areas lacking a top grade ask yourself where you would look for answers.

4. Start asking friends for their suggestions on advisors. Also inquire if those they recommend are good listeners and communicators and whether they are trustworthy.

5. Follow the suggestions in this Lesson in picking advisors.

Mark's Story

When I was young we lived in Southern California where the grass grows all year. It was my job to mow the lawn every week – a task that I loathed. After I left home for college and moved into student housing, I no longer had a lawn to mow and was thrilled. Things stayed that way until, when married with young children, we decided to get a home in suburban Virginia, which had a large lawn needing regular care. So I was back to taking care of the yard.

One day, as I was getting ready to mow the lawn, which at this point, was taking me a few hours every precious weekend, a young man walked up and offered to mow, edge and clean up for me. I asked him how much and he said $35. I thought about it for about two seconds and agreed. He then brought out an industrial ride-behind mower and proceeded to cut my lawn better than I ever had in about ten minutes. He then took out an equally industrial-sized edger/trimmer and did a great job finishing the sides, and then cleaned up everything using other specialty equipment. All told, it took him about half an hour to do the job, and he did it far better than I could hope even, if I spent all day.

I hired him and his company still does all my lawn care. That decision made my life considerably easier in several ways:

- It was a job I disliked and was not very good at anyway. Now I have a professional who enjoys this work and does it well.

- There were many weekends when it was very inconvenient for me to do yard work either because of travel or other obligations. Now, instead of my yard looking shabby, the work gets done at the right time so it always looks good.

- There were many weekends when the weather did not permit yard work. Now, the work gets done as soon as possible, and I do not have to be there to make it happen.

I have a neighbor who is older, retired and likes nothing more than to work on his yard. Every time I pass by his house, he is outside. He's doing he wants with his ample spare time and his yard looks OK, although I think mine is more consistently groomed.

My fee for consulting services is considerable. If I were to pay myself the minimum of two hours that it takes to mow the lawn, I would in effect be losing over two billable hours in value, not to mention doing something I disliked and missing time with my family. Hiring a lawn service was one of the smartest financial decisions I ever made.

Take This to the Bank

- You can't do everything yourself. Seek the advice of experts when you need help.

- Make sure you find someone you trust. If your instincts warn you against that person, look elsewhere.

- Find listeners. Does the advisor want to know about your problems or concerns or does he seem more interested in showing you how much he knows? Who is doing the talking?

- Find good communicators. How often does your financial planner communicate with clients and how – through email, letter, newsletter, town hall meetings, seminars, or all of these? Does the attorney send out updates on estate planning and other areas of concern and personalized letters alerting you to changes in the law?

- If the prospective investment advisor or salesperson dodges the question of fees by changing the subject when you bring it up, politely tell them you are not interested and leave.

Parting Shot

How you use your money tomorrow is **tactical**; what you do with it over time is **strategic**. Those who only think and act tactically are only dealing with the short term and lack of planning may put them in dire straits. Knowledgeable and experienced advisors can teach you new and innovative ways to strategically prepare for the future.

You can choose your advisors individually or opt for one-stop shopping, integrated advice on legal, tax, financial and risk management. Regardless of which way you go, look for strategists who are more than scorekeepers. Seek advisors who will put your interests ahead of their own. A good advisor will earn his or her fee many times over.

LESSON 10

Being Organized
Pays Dividends

The average American spends about an hour a day
looking for misplaced items.

If you are organized, not only can you be creative and pursue your goals without the clutter, mess, and the distraction of searching for lost objects but you get back that hour, less the five or so minutes it takes to stay organized. Imagine what you can do with six and a half extra hours a week!

Keeping your papers and records organized also saves you money. You promptly deposit checks, respond to correspondence, and pay bills on time. You can avoid late charges and an impaired credit record. Things that are now big ordeals, like preparing your income taxes or doing a financial statement for a mortgage application, are much easier and simpler.

Finally, being organized allows you to plan ahead instead of constantly playing catch-up. It will save you time, money, stress, and allows you to focus on where you want to go instead of trying to figure out where you are.

Why Be Organized?

Being organized is not just something you do; it is a way of life. It applies to your home, work, papers and records, and time. While not particularly complicated, being organized will take some effort on your part. Rather than being instinctive or intuitive, organization is a skill that needs to be learned.

The first step towards becoming organized is to **keep good records.** This means having checks, receipts, and other paperwork in a specific place ordered by specific topics so you can easily locate the desired information. Recordkeeping separates the winners from the losers in billing battles. If you like to win, then keep the papers to prove it. Documentation is how you get paid for your claims, how you get your refund, and how you prove you were right and some company wrong. Having a good filing system also gives you peace of mind since you can always find the paper you need and your tax returns and other tasks are more readily handled.

It's especially important to maintain good records regarding tax matters. While the IRS is very thorough in tracking all your sources of income, they could care less whether you report any deductions. So it is up to you to not only keep good records of your income but also of all payments and expenses that could help you save money on your taxes. If you can't prove your deduction and you get audited, then you will have to pay the extra tax, interest, and penalties.

What Should You Organize?

Your time. Your time is your most precious resource. Guard it carefully and avoid waste by planning ahead. The best way to organize your time is by using a calendar and checklists:

1. Keep a *calendar* for your appointments and deadlines. You can use a calendar from a basic computer program such as Microsoft Outlook or a "smart phone" like an iPhone, BlackBerry or Palm. Even many inexpensive cell phones have a calendar. Or you can use a low-tech paper calendar that has social, sports, and other family-related appointments. However, make sure to check any calendars you use and consolidate them into a single schedule. That way, you will avoid time conflicts and missing appointments.

2. Use *checklists* so you know what you need to do every day. Checklists and prioritizing are discussed in Lesson 4. They will help make sure that you keep and make all your appointments, deadlines, and obligations and will greatly simplify your life.

Be on time for your appointments. Being late is disrespectful of another's time and can get you started on the wrong foot. By the same token, stay away from others who are habitually late. They have little respect for time – theirs and yours – and are themselves disorganized. Finally, by being organized and on time, you earn the reputation as a dependable person whom others can trust.

Tax-related papers. Three categories of tax-related papers should be set aside.

1. *Income.* Keep all papers showing your income for the year. This does not mean every pay stub, just the income reporting form(s) that your employer, bank and (if applicable) investment company sends you early each year. These are forms W-2s, 1099s, or K-1s. However, if you have worked for several different places and earned under $600 they may not send you a form. So, to be safe, keep records of payment from each of these places in event you do not receive an IRS form.

2. *Expenses.* Only certain expenses are **deductible**; that is, they can be counted against your income so you pay lower taxes. Therefore, you only need to keep track of the deductible expenses.

3. *Cost Basis Information.* When you sell an asset you might be selling it for more than you paid, in which case you have a **gain,** or for less than you paid, in which case you have a **loss**. So you need to keep track of what you initially paid for your investment assets; that is, the **tax basis.**

All papers should be kept in manila folders and labeled by type and date. For example, with taxes, keep pertinent forms and papers in folders marked "Income" "Deductions" and "Asset Sales and Basis" with the tax year. If you put them all in a file cabinet and alphabetize them, then you'll be able to get to them easily. Another option would be to scan them on your computer and back them up on another hard drive or the cloud – an online backup storage center – or both. Regardless of how you organize your documents, keep them in a safe, secure place and make duplicates as an extra precaution.

Receipts and warranties. Keep the receipts and warranties for at least as long as the warranty period and if the item is insured, until you no longer own the item. If the item is damaged or lost in such a way that it's covered by insurance, the receipt will help prove the claim. Repairs often come with warranties so keep paperwork relating to those as well.

Loan related papers. Even though these are also typically stored online by most financial institutions, it's a good idea to have these in your files, especially if you need to refinance your house or car. You never know what papers or information may help you secure a better rate or loan.

Important personal papers. These papers should be kept in a secure place, safe from fire, theft, or damage. Either a fire safe at home or a safe deposit box at a bank will do. They include:

- Diplomas, passport, military discharge papers, marriage certificate, birth certificate, medical records

- If you have them, estate planning papers – wills, trusts, powers of attorney, medical directives

- Also if you have them, investment papers such as stock certificates, certificates of insurance, and CDs

All income sources and all recurring expenses. With good budget software you will already be gathering this information (see Lesson 3 on budgeting). Keep records of bills and other expenses for a year. In many cases, however, banks and credit card companies maintain records of your payments and purchases online for several months, so even this may not be necessary.

What Should You Get Rid of?

Anyone who's ever seen the TV program "Hoarders" knows how scary and dangerous keeping every single piece of paper or item you've ever owned can be. Not only does it constitute a safety hazard but it results in disorganization to the point of chaos. So it's just as important to know what **not** to keep. This includes:

- Anything that you can readily find online, whether on a secure or public site. The Internet is a veritable goldmine of information that includes back issues of magazines, newspapers, and other written material; bank, brokerage, and credit card statements; utility bills and account statements; and operating manuals and instructions. Having such information online eliminates the necessity for paper records.

- Anything that is kept by another. The official copy of the deed to your house, for example, is on record at the courthouse. The original signed deed in your safe deposit box is not needed by anyone. When you go to sell your house, the prospective buyer (their title insurance company, actually) will go to the courthouse and make sure you own the house. They will not even ask for your deed. Unlike mortgage information, which you may need indefinitely and only you may have access to, the deed can always be retrieved from the court house.

Mark's Story

I like to putter around in my woodworking shop at home and I subscribe to several woodworker magazines. For years I have been keeping these magazines in the shop and they were taking up a lot of space. Recently I noticed that the publisher is selling a CD with electronic copies of all the magazines published by them for the past 25 years. I jumped on it in a heartbeat. For about $30 I was able to replace two shelves of dusty magazines with a much more useful indexed and searchable DVD.

- Anything you can scan and keep on your computer. Invest in a scanner so you can store your papers electronically. Make sure you also have a reliable backup system, preferably something cloud-based that allows you to recover easily from a total electronic loss in your house (think fire or water damage).

When it comes to accumulating paper and killing trees, not to mention minimizing your carbon footprint, less is definitely more.

Mark and Wes' Story

Several years ago, our firm had about 7,000 client files and we spent over an hour a day looking for and retrieving them. In addition, we paid substantial fees to store and fetch the less active files offsite. So we digitized all files and shredded the paper, over one million sheets! Now we can find any file instantly and reliably in our computer systems. We also have a robust backup system with information stored in multiple locations.

How to Start Organizing

You cannot organize your entire life all at once. Do it one step at a time. So start by determining exactly what it is (the scope) you'd like to organize. Your desk, books, or study area? Your bedroom? Your clothing and shoes? Your calendar and how you spend your time? Once you have identified the scope, all organizing projects follow the same four steps:

1.   *Sort.* First, go through all the items you are organizing and put them in categories that work for you. (This is **your** system, so the categories do not have to make sense to anyone else). For example, if you are organizing your DVD collection, you might do it alphabetically by name or producer, or you might organize the DVDs by movie category such as Westerns, romance, children's, action/adventure, etc. Keep it simple. Using as few categories as possible makes it much easier to retrieve whatever you might be looking for in the future.

2.   *Discard.* Then as you sort through your stuff, get rid of things you don't really need. Has it outgrown its usefulness and sentimental value? Have you even thought about it in the past two years? Does it still fit? Can you get the information online?

3.   *Assign.* Assign a home for each thing you are keeping. Be specific so that you will know exactly where to return the item when you are done using it. Use a simple labeling machine to produce neat and attractive labels that will stick. Store things in containers. The storage solutions should be logical and help your with your workflow. For example, put all printing supplies (paper, toner, cartridges)

near the printer or store seasonal clothing in a large plastic bin that will prevent them from becoming wrinkled and smelly. Sentimental items – things you no longer use but cannot bear to let go – can be placed in a box labeled "Memorabilia." Later, when you want to relive memories you'll know exactly where to find them.

4. *Maintain.* Putting away and adding new things should take no more than five minutes a day. But maintaining the system is just as important as the other steps; otherwise, all your organizing efforts are for nothing.

At first you may find organizing somewhat intimidating. So ask for help from family, friends, or even a teacher or mentor. If you're really challenged with organizing you might want to seek out a professional organizer (See Lesson 9 on advisors).

As time passes, you may find that your current system no longer meets your needs. Life is full of changes – marriage, a baby, a new job, or a move – and these may have an effect on how you organize things. Whenever there is a change, evaluate the various systems to make sure they are still effective. There's nothing wrong with switching things up and tweaking them to meet your specific needs. The goal is to work smarter, not adhere to a particular way of doing things.

The Organizer's Toolbox

What follows are some essentials that will help you get – and stay – organized.

- A worksheet. This can be as simple as a lined tablet or purchasing inexpensive (or sometimes free!) system from specialized Websites such as www.onlineorganizing.com or www.lifeorganizers.com. Free financial checklists can be found at www.aarp.org/money/personal/articles/ FinancialPlanningOrganizing.html.

- Computer with folders set up to hold scanned or electronic copies of bills and other documents

- Scanner or access to a scanner

- File cabinet

- File folders

- Labels and/or a label maker

- Staples

- Paperclips or clasps

- Hole punch

Additional suggestions

- If you keep your records in folders, file the most recent statement in front or on top and oldest underneath. Do this daily or as soon as the bill has been paid. This will ensure that papers do not get lost or misplaced.

- Clearly labeled, file folders should follow a sequence matching your budget and asset categories. This can also be done on your computer; clearly label each electronic file so you can find it by topic and date.

- If you have them, keep all statements, including medical directives, powers of attorneys, and net worth statements in a clearly designated folder.

Make sure someone knows where such information can be found in case of unexpected death or incapacity.

- Have a running list of the contents of your house either in writing or by video in the event of substantial property damage or loss due to fire, theft, water and so on. You can walk around the house and photograph or videotape the contents of each room. Revise the list annually by adding major purchases or any changes.

- Keep a tax files for each year, one labeled "income," the other labeled "deductions," and so forth. Throughout the year, keep adding to those files so that at tax time you already have all the information collected.

- Keep a file for receipts and warranties. Big items, like your car, deserve their own file.

How Long Should You Keep Items?

The statute of limitations for income tax returns is three years but in some cases can be as long as six years. This means that the IRS will not be interested in any tax return information that is more than six years old – that is, from the date of that you filed it. To be safe, keep all tax records, and a copy of the tax return itself for six years. You can scan all income tax papers and keep them on the computer (and several backups as well). Only then can you shred your tax papers.

Other things that should be kept indefinitely include:

- Cost basis information on assets until they are sold and even then it should be made a part of the tax file for the year of sale.

- Mortgage information, until the mortgage is paid off and the property sold. Even then you should retain a copy of the certificate of satisfaction to make sure it does not show up on a credit report, on a title search as unpaid, or as a source of concern about an IRS review of the sale.

- Service agreement until the service is terminated, all bills are paid and there are no outstanding service issues. Easiest way to do this is to mark each agreement with a "Discard After [Date]."

- Receipts (or credit/debit card bills that show purchases) in case you have to make warranty claims or you have damage such as a house fire and must claim the value of the items destroyed.

You should also keep records on these items until the following conditions are met:

- *Car.* Until you sell the car, plus an additional year in case the buyer fails to retitle the car and you have to prove sale.

- *Insurance policies and related papers.* Until you cancel the policy, all claims are resolved, and the policy has expired without a claim.

- *Receipts for significant purchases* such as a television, MP3 player, cell phone, and others until you no longer own them so you can prove ownership and value in case of damage or defect.

TIP FOR THE PARENT: The parents gave their son notebooks at a very young age and encouraged him to use them. He recorded his thoughts and experiences in a diary and learned the value of keeping track. The same was true for his homework. Later, he was in scouting, where they have checklists for everything. He later joined the Navy. The Navy's checklists were longer. Learning the organizational lesson while he was young, he will never lack for organization of his papers.

Take This to the Bank

- Follow the one-touch rule. Whenever possible, take care of a matter the first time you touch it. If you open a bill, pay it right then. If you open a letter, reply right then. It will save a lot of time and you will develop the reputation of an organized and efficient person.

- Do the hard things first. Although it's normal to want to put off a difficult task, you will likely be agonizing over it, which can distract from other things you need to be doing. So dealing with it directly will help put your mind at ease and often turns out to be less intimidating than you originally thought.

- When in doubt, save all financial documentation in paper or electronic form. If you use electronic records, have a good backup system and also a good safeguard against identify theft.

- In discarding records, shred them, rather than throwing them in the trash can.

- Go to the office supply store if you do not have the materials to get organized. Even purchasing a few items will provide you with incentive to go home and start sorting.

Parting Shot

Recordkeeping is essential to your financial security and safety. Even those with a photographic memory cannot use personal recollection to prove a claim, get a refund or otherwise triumph in any battle over money with another, such as the IRS. Nor can you put together a budget, come up with a savings plan, or assemble and track a net worth statement without physical records.

But keeping good records is just one aspect of being organized. If you are organized, you will have more balance in your life. You'll minimize the time spent on necessary things like shopping and searching for misplaced items, but increase the time spent on important things like family and hobbies.

So try to make being organized a way of life. The sooner you start, the sooner it will be a habit and the more quickly you'll reap the benefits.

LESSON 11

Ask What Your Taxes
Can Do For You

I am proud to pay taxes to the United States; the only thing is,
I could be just as proud for half the money.

Arthur Godfrey

Many decisions you make in life have tax implications. Marriage, divorce, buying or selling a house, having a child, getting a job, even contributing to your retirement plan or portfolio all have tax consequences. You'll need to understand, for example, the difference between cashing in your 401(k) when you quit your job (bad choice tax-wise) versus rolling it into an IRA (much better tax-wise), or the difference between a gift to a friend (not deductible) versus a contribution to a charity (deductible if you itemize).

So even if you never prepare your own income tax returns, you'll need a basic understanding of tax rules. Since you can't consult with your tax professional about every single life change, you should become somewhat knowledgeable about taxes; if nothing more than to know when to ask for help to avoid trouble with the IRS.

There are many different kinds of taxes – income tax, sales tax, excise tax, property tax, FICA tax, Medicare tax, alternative minimum tax, gift tax, estate tax, and more. This Lesson will focus on just the basics of the federal income tax.

Organizing Your Taxes

At minimum, you'll need a tax file or shoe box to store all your tax-related papers throughout the year This includes pay slips, charitable contributions, child care expenses, medical expenses, and so on. The truly efficient can subdivide expenses and put them into separate folders, saving time and effort in sorting these papers into relevant piles when tax season rolls around.

In January and February you will be getting a Form W-2 from your employer summarizing your wages and withholdings, as well as a Form 1099 or Form K-1 for each bank account, loan, and investment. All of these should also go into your tax file. By late February or early March you should have all your tax information collected and be able to fill out your own income tax return or take it to a professional preparer, unless you know of missing information such as K-1s.

You report your income by filing Form 1040 (see Tax Talk box on the next page) or one of its variations, depending on the complexity of your situation. Your income taxes are paid over the course of the year through withholding from your wages and/or quarterly estimated payments. The due date for the return and any remaining tax owed is April 15. The filing of the full return can be extended, but not the tax payment. It will always be due no later than April 15, and if you fail to pay it by then, you will likely be subject to penalties and interest.

Tax Talk

Along with *Form 1040*, the standard individual tax return form of the IRS (or variations of the 1040, depending upon your situation and how and when you file), you may need one or more of the following IRS forms when filing your taxes.

- *Form W-2* (also known as the *Wage and Tax Statement*). Each employer must provide their employers with a Form W-2 showing total wages, federal income tax withheld, FICA (Social Security) taxes withheld, state taxes withheld and other pertinent information. The employee then files the W-2 with his or her Form 1040.

- *Form 1099.* Form 1099 is used to report a variety of unique income payments to the IRS, including part-time and contract work; dividend payments from a mutual fund, company, or other investment; interest payments from a bank, bond fund, or other investment; capital gains proceeds; and rents, royalties and miscellaneousincome. Each 1099 reflects the sum of that source of income payments for the year.

- *Schedule K-1.* Schedule K-1 is used to report a beneficiary's or partner's share of income, deductions, credits, and other items from limited partnerships, corporations, trusts, and limited liability companies. For example, if you had an interest in Company XYZ partnership and received $1,000 of income from the partnership last year, your K-1 would reflect that income and you would pay taxes on it with your tax return.

Once your return is completed and sent in, you'll want to save a signed copy of the return and all the supporting papers for six years.

Mark's Story

I have a file box where I store my returns. It holds six years' worth of returns (federal and state) and every year I add the most recent return and remove and shred the oldest one. I also started storing the returns electronically and can keep them indefinitely.

However, unless fraud is suspected, the IRS cannot ask for an income tax return that was filed on time and is more than six years old, and in many cases, cannot ask for one more than three years old.

Income

The rules for determining taxable income can get quite complicated. Some basics are described in the following paragraphs.

There are two types of taxable income: Ordinary income and capital gains. **Ordinary income** includes things like wages, bonuses, tips, interest, rents, royalties, dividends and most amounts being paid out of an IRA or a qualified plan. Ordinary income is generally taxed at a higher rate than capital gains, and the more ordinary income you have the higher the tax rate. This is known as a **progressive tax**. You also have limited opportunities to control the timing of when you incur the income and limited ability to deduct losses against ordinary income. Ordinary income is the most taxed and least favored of taxable income.

Capital gains are a tax on the increase in the value of an asset held for investment, and are paid the year the asset is sold. Capital gains are usually taxed at a flat rate which is usually significantly lower than ordinary income tax. Capital assets held for a long time (usually more than a year) are taxed at a lower flat rate than those held for a shorter term. Unlike ordinary income, you can control the timing of when you will pay the tax by deciding when to sell. If the asset is sold at a loss, the amount lost can offset the gains from other capital assets sold in the same year (or in later years) reducing the overall capital gains tax. There is also a limited capital loss offset ($3,000 per year) against ordinary income, which means up to $3,000 of your capital loss is deducted from your taxable income (and you pay less taxes). Tax law clearly favors income from capital gains over ordinary income.

Tax rules are different for self-employed people and business owners. Unlike salaried workers, they pay taxes on their net income – what they actually get from their clients and/or for providing a product or service, less their expenses – and must be very careful to put aside money for taxes, insurance and so forth, so they don't get caught short. So if you have a job working in restaurant, where tips make up most of your salary, be sure to put aside enough for taxes and keep good records.

Cost Basis Information

Basis, sometimes referred to as **cost basis**, is used to keep track of your taxable gains or losses and in a simple case, is what you initially paid for the asset. If you bought ABC stock for $10 and later sold it for $15, your basis is $10 and your **gain** is the sales price minus the basis, or $5. However, some cases are more complicated. Say you bought a rental property for $100,000 (cost basis), put a new roof on it for $10,000, held it for five years and then sold it for $150,000. You "depreciate" the value of the house using the IRS schedule which equals, say, approximately $3,000 per year for the five years, a total of $15,000. The depreciation deduction offset your income each year by the $3,000 and saved you some taxes. However, it also reduced your basis in the property by $3,000 per year for five years. So your basis after depreciation is now $85,000. The cost of the new roof (a "capital improvement") is added to basis, so, after the new roof (plus $10K) and five years of depreciation (minus $15K) your basis is $95,000. Your taxable gain on the sale is $55,000 – the $150,000 sales price minus the basis of $95,000. (Some of your gain is characterized as "recapture of depreciation" and is taxed at the recapture rates.)

Non-Income Items

Not everything is counted as taxable income. Money received as a gift or inheritance is not taxable income, but any earnings you would make from that money is. Life insurance proceeds paid to you by reason of the death of the insured is not taxable income. Also, interest from municipal bonds is not income for federal taxes, but might be for state taxes. Some employer-paid benefits, such as healthcare or group-term life insurance, are not considered income. Finally, money contributed by your employer to a qualified retirement plan is subtracted from your taxable wages and only taxed later when it is distributed from the retirement plan.

Deductions and Credits

Deductions reduce your income which reduces your tax. Everyone is entitled to a **personal exemption** of $3,650 in 2009, unless someone else is claiming you as a dependent. If you have large enough amount of the expenses listed below, you can **itemize** or list them on your return. Otherwise, you will use a **standard deduction**, a fixed amount allowed to taxpayers who do not itemize.

What to Deduct?

Expenses. Only certain expenses are deductible and you need to keep track of the deductible expenses. The most common ones include:

- Medical expenses that are high in proportion to your adjusted gross income (more than 7.5 percent)

- Mortgage interest
- Charitable contributions
- State and local tax payments (including personal property taxes in some cases)
- Real estate property tax payments
- Investment fees
- Tax preparation expenses

This is only a partial list and the items are subject to limitations. Deductions can be quite complicated, so you may need to seek the advice of a tax expert or accountant to make sure they are correct.

If you do not have enough deductions to itemize, you can use the **standard deduction** illustrated in Figure 11.1. Of course, the amount will be different for each tax year.

Single	$5,700
Head of Household	$8,350
Married Filing Joint	$11,400
Married Filing Separately	$5,700

Figure 11.1 Standard Deduction for 2009

If your itemized deductions exceed your standard deduction, you will want to itemize them on Schedule A of your return.

Above-the-Line Deductions. Above-the-line deductions are valuable because they can reduce your gross income to arrive at the **adjusted gross income (AGI)**. They can be used even if you do not itemize your deductions. They are generally not subject to phase-outs for higher income taxpayers. Examples include alimony payments, clean fuel vehicles, moving expenses, interest on student loans, higher education expenses, retirement plan savings for the self-employed, and health savings accounts. Learn about these deductions and try to arrange to qualify for them.

Credits. Credits reduce your tax directly. You may be entitled to credits against your tax such as the "child and dependent care" credit or the earned income credit (EIC) or the "first time home buyer" credit. These credits are valuable if you have a tax due, since they reduce the tax dollar for dollar.

Tales of Tax Terror: Two Arguments for Consulting the Experts

Lesson 9 discusses building your circle of experts. Since taxes have such a big impact on your life, you need to be especially careful when choosing an accountant, tax lawyer, or financial tax expert. It's far better to spend a few hundred dollars to have your taxes filed correctly and on time than to skimp and try to do them yourself. Any mistake in this area can have life-changing implications and despite its efforts to promote itself as benevolent; the IRS is still a pretty scary prospect.

Ben's Story

A recent college graduate, Ben decided to save money by doing his tax return online and completed it incorrectly. He submitted it to the IRS, then several months later realized he might have made a mistake when they wrote him back asking him for more information about his charitable deductions. To help resolve the situation, he needed to locate his old return which he neglected to print out or save to his computer. He ended up writing the charities and asking for letters of verification as well as frantically searching his bank records for copies of cancelled checks as well as credit card payments and debit deductions. Months went by before be wrapped up the matter with lots of energy, money, and penalties (for underpaying his taxes). He was very stressed during this period. Going to a tax expert with knowledge of such matters would have made his life much easier.

Peter's Story

When his father passed away unexpectedly, Peter inherited his individual retirement account (IRA.) He figured that the easiest and least expensive option would be to roll over the money into his own IRA. So he asked his broker to do so, assuming that the broker also knew about inheritance taxes and IRAs since he was in charge of Peter's financial affairs. Wrong! When tax season rolled around and Peter went to his tax preparer, he discovered that putting the IRA in his name alone instead of as an inherited IRA with his dad's name meant that not only did he have to pay all the income taxes on his dad's IRA that year but also he also had to pay penalties for improperly funding his IRA. So he took a big hit and was forced to take money out of savings to pay for the penalties. It was a very expensive lesson and now that his affairs are more complicated, he uses a financial advisor with experience in investing, retirement, and taxes.

TIP FOR THE PARENT: The daughter recalled: As a child, Dad did our tax forms every year and then insisted on going over the forms with us, instead of just signing it and sending it in. I've heard the story many times that as a young child I was going over these forms with my dad and there were taxes to the state of Tennessee (as a military family we could declare residency in the state of our choice). I suppose that I had very few taxes, my existing income was all from stocks. I am told I said: "I have to pay taxes to Tennessee?!? I've never even BEEN to Tennessee." I learned about taxes early on as well as record keeping.

Take This to the Bank

- All major life decisions have tax implications.

- Store all tax information in a safe place and keep it for six years.

- Understand the tax differences between self-employed and salaried workers, as you may be both in your lifetime.

- The more you know about taxes, the more you'll be able to deduct and save.

- Always report and pay your taxes on time.

- Unless your taxes are extremely simple, consider using a licensed and reputable tax preparer.

Parting Shot

Everyone is responsible for reporting his/her income by filing an income tax return and paying their taxes. Ignorance of the law is not an excuse. If you do not properly report and pay then you will owe interest on the late taxes and perhaps penalties as well. You might even go to jail – tax fraud is a crime. Intentionally not reporting all your income is also considered tax fraud.

CONCLUSION

Make Your Money
Work for You

*Happiness is the meaning and the purpose of life, the whole
aim and end of human existence.*

Aristotle

Financial independence is critical to your own well-being. Being financially independent is not the same as being extraordinarily rich – the media is full of stories about millionaires and wealthy celebrities who have a host of problems. Nor does it mean you can spend as much you'd like. Rather, it means freedom from worry about finances.

Financial independence can take many forms. Some of our clients have and earn very little but have a wonderful home or residence paid for in full, a good family life, good food, their medical care covered, and savings in the bank. Their lives are relatively free of financial worries, because what money they have is working for them, rather than the other way around.

Thanks to the recent recession, the home mortgage crisis, and new and stricter credit card laws, Americans are slowly coming around to a different way of thinking; that is, living within their means and saving. The following checklists illustrate points covered in the Lessons and will help make sure that you are staying on track with your finances as well.

How Can I Tell If My Money Is Working Against Me?

- You are constantly worrying about making ends meet.

- You are living paycheck to paycheck with no plan.

- Everything is going out the door to meet expenses.

- You spend more than you make.

- You are taking out an equity line of credit on your house to buy necessities and pay bills.

- You have no financial plan, savings, budget, or net worth statement.

How Can I Tell If My Money Is Working for Me?

- It is coming back to you at some point through investment, retirement accounts, or education that pays you dividends in the future.

- You are saving 10 percent per year.

- You are maxing out on all retirement savings options and building up your Roth, 401(k), and other investments.

- Your portfolio is diversified, with stocks, bonds, securities and other investments from both the United States and the rest of the world.

- You are continuing to invest time and money in knowledge that will continue to pave your road to success.

- You are using the services of strategic advisors who have your best interests at heart.

How Can I Make My Money Work for Me?

- Start learning as much as you can about financial literacy now.

- Learn how to balance a checkbook.

- Learn how to prepare a net worth statement.

- Set up a budget and stick to it.

- Allocate each dollar to an expense or savings category.

- Cut your expenses and live within your means.

- Track it and adjust the budget with changed circumstances.

- Stay out of debt.

- When saving:

  - Start now and never stop.

  - Save at least 10 percent.

- When investing:

  - Check out expenses for each investment. What are you paying for? Is it worth that much to you?

- Make sure you are getting value for your money.

- Check your emotions at the door. Purchases should be reasoned and logical.

- Do not put all of your investment eggs in one company or stock. Diversify with other kinds of investments.

Last but Not Least...

Invest in yourself. Have you always wanted to start a business or pursue a career that you love? What is holding you back? Get going. Get the education and instruction needed, work nights and weekends, give it a go and make sure it is viable before you leave the comfort of your job to jump off the financial cliff. On the other hand, if you already fell over the cliff when you were let go by our old employer, then jump right in and go for it!

Regardless of what happens, if you plan ahead, you'll hopefully have the investment money needed as well as your own emergency or rainy day fund.

In the journey of life, each person has their own separate path. Financial well-being hardly guarantees happiness, but it does provide a very strong foundation for an enjoyable life. The rest is up to you.

About the Authors

I. Mark Cohen, J.D., LL.M, CFP®

I. Mark Cohen, J.D., LL.M, CFP® is the founding partner and visionary for both Navigator Wealth Management, LLC, Registered Investment Advisor, and Cohen & Burnett, P.C., Attorneys and Counselors at Law. His mission is to demonstrate the superior results of a multidisciplinary approach to wealth management.

Mark is licensed to practice law in both Virginia and Arizona. He is a registered representative of Pacific West Securities, Inc., an independent broker/dealer. Mark is a past president of the Northern Virginia Estate Planning Council and is an active member of the Legislative Committee of the Wills Trusts and Estates Section of the Virginia State Bar Association. Mark is a frequent lecturer and writer at attorney CLE seminars where he specializes in estate taxes and ethics.

Mark has been published extensively in trusts and estates

journals and magazines, and is the author of the first and only comprehensive treatise on the Uniform Trust Code, (Cohen, 864 T.M. 1st, Uniform Trust Code). To learn more about Mark's law and wealth management firms and publications, please visit: www.navigatorwealth.com and www.cohenandburnett.com.

Mark grew up in an Air Force family the son of a rocket scientist. He has lived in Ohio, Colorado, California, Israel, Arizona and Virginia. He met his wife, Kathy, during his first year of law school while she was working on her Masters in Teaching English as a Second Language. Together they have two children, Michael and Rachel, who are both undergraduate students at the College of William and Mary.

Mark enjoys woodworking, guitar, and anything that gets him outdoors, especially cycling, kayaking, flying small airplanes, sailing, and backpacking.

Weston D. Burnett, J.D., LL.M, CFP®

Weston D. Burnett, J.D., LL.M, CFP®, is the Managing Partner of Cohen & Burnett, PC, Attorneys and Counselors at Law and President and CEO of Navigator Wealth Management, LLC. He helps his clients and their families realize their life goals and gain peace-of-mind by espousing an integrated, strategic approach to legal, tax, and financial planning.

Wes is a 1972 cum laude graduate of Vanderbilt University with a Bachelor of Arts Degree in History, Philosophy and Political Science. He subsequently graduated with Honors in 1975 from George Washington University Law School. That same year, he was admitted to the practice of law in Virginia and entered on active duty with the Navy as a judge advocate. In

1983, he earned a Masters of Law Degree with Highest Honors in International and Comparative Law at George Washington University Law School. He retired from the Navy as a senior captain in May 2000 and joined I. Mark Cohen's law practice. He has since been admitted to the practice of law in Maryland and the District of Columbia. In September 2003, he became a Certified Financial Planner®. Wes has been published over the last three decades in a wide variety of subject areas.

Wes grew up in a Navy family and has lived on three continents and moved over 25 times in his life. He married Barbara Feicht within a week of her graduation from Vanderbilt University with Cum Laude honors in 1973. They have three children: David, Edward, and Jennifer.

Wes Burnett is proud to serve in various alumni leadership roles with George Washington University and its Law School. He enjoys running, hiking, biking, golf, skiing, stamp collecting, history, military affairs, and family and friends.

OUR FORMULA FOR PEACE OF MIND IS SIMPLE.

LEGAL + TAX + FINANCIAL PLANNING = INTEGRATED STRATEGIES

Navigator Wealth Management's holistic approach to wealth management, strict adherence to the highest of ethics, and commitment to act as fiduciaries in each client's best interest is what sets us apart from brokers or others who sell you products or simply invest your money.

NAVIGATOR™

WEALTH MANAGEMENT

INTEGRATED STRATEGIES. PEACE OF MIND.

www.navigatorwealth.com

Navigator Wealth Management, LLC,
is a Registered Investment Advisory Firm (RIA).